T0243853

DON'T FOLLOW YOUR HEART

DON'T FOLLOW YOUR HEART

BOLDLY BREAKING THE TEN COMMANDMENTS OF SELF-WORSHIP

THADDEUS J. WILLIAMS

WITH THE VOICES OF JONI EARECKSON TADA, THE NAVARROS,
JAMAL BANDY, J. P. MORELAND, JOSH MCDOWELL, ALYSSA POBLETE,
TREVOR WRIGHT, DAVID CHUNG, ALISA CHILDERS, AND WALT HEYER

ZONDERVAN
REFLECTIVE

ZONDERVAN REFLECTIVE

Don't Follow Your Heart
Copyright © 2023 by Thaddeus J. Williams

Requests for information should be addressed to:
Zondervan, *3900 Sparks Dr. SE, Grand Rapids, Michigan 49546*

Zondervan titles may be purchased in bulk for educational, business, fundraising, or sales promotional use. For information, please email SpecialMarkets@Zondervan.com.

ISBN 978-0-310-15450-1 (audio)

Library of Congress Cataloging-in-Publication Data

Names: Williams, Thaddeus J., author.
Title: Don't follow your heart : boldly breaking the ten commandments of self-worship / Thaddeus J. Williams.
Description: Grand Rapids : Zondervan, 2023. | Includes index.
Identifiers: LCCN 2023013001 (print) | LCCN 2023013002 (ebook) | ISBN 9780310154464 (paperback) | ISBN 9780310154495 (ebook)
Subjects: LCSH: Self—Religious aspects—Christianity. | Popular culture—Religious aspects—Christianity. | Identity (Psychology)—Religious aspects—Christianity. | Christian sociology. | BISAC: RELIGION / Christian Living / Social Issues | SOCIAL SCIENCE / Popular Culture
Classification: LCC BT713 .W55 2023 (print) | LCC BT713 (ebook) | DDC 248.4—dc23/eng/20230512
LC record available at https://lccn.loc.gov/2023013001
LC ebook record available at https://lccn.loc.gov/2023013002

Cover design: Charles Brock, Brock Book Design Co.
Cover art: © Marcink3333 / Depositphotos
Interior design: Denise Froehlich
Dove on p. 128: bazilfoto / iStockphoto.com

Printed in the United States of America

23 24 25 26 27 28 29 30 31 32 33 /TRM/ 15 14 13 12 11 10 9 8 7 6 5 4 3 2 1

Dedication

My daughter Holland, "Dutch" for short, was nine years old. For years, we had played a game together called Spot the Lie. The rules were simple enough. If she could spot a lie—identify a false idea and explain why it was false—in whatever show we were watching, whatever YouTube clip, whatever movie, she would earn a dollar. She and her siblings got so good at it, part of me thought I'd be living in a cardboard box before too long.

"Daddy, daddy," she said, cheerfully bounding down the stairs, "You owe me another dollar!" "What did you find this time, Dutch?" She had just seen an ad for a new pink pixie fairy princess unicorn doll or whatever. "The commercial told me I should follow my heart." "OK, so where's the lie?" I asked. Her answer will forever live in the file in my mind marked "Ultimate Parenting Wins." Her answer, and I recall it verbatim, was, "Daddy, I don't want to follow my own heart. My heart is fallen. I'd way rather follow God's heart. It's way better!" Cue the proud daddy tears. Let's just say she earned five dollars for that one.

Some may think, "What a shame—he's indoctrinating that poor girl." The opposite is true. I'm trying to make a heretic out of her. I want her to question and ultimately rebel against the doctrines of our day. Indeed, we need an entire generation of heretics, iconoclasts, renegades, mavericks, and rebels who refuse to march like good little cows, mooing in unison with the herd. When advertisers, TikTok influencers, singing princesses, pop star divas, animated potatoes, and university professors tell them to be true to themselves, find the answers within, and follow their hearts, they say, "To hell with your dogma!" To Dutch and a new generation of heretics, I affectionately dedicate this book.

Contents

Foreword

We've all had the feeling that life just isn't as satisfying as it should be. We've all felt alienated from others, from the universe, even from ourselves. Alienation has been a shared experience throughout human history, but in our day it comes with an intensity that leaves us with a kind of existential vertigo. We have become untethered from the transcendent sources of meaning that helped so many of our ancestors orient themselves in the world.

Traditional Christianity told men and women that they are created in the image of God and that the chief end of our existence is to worship and enjoy God forever. On this view, we are profoundly dependent on something or rather Someone beyond ourselves to tap into the meaning of life, namely, our Creator. As this Christian vision lost its grip on the cultural imagination in the West, its notions of dependence and obligation beyond ourselves remained central. Even after the Enlightenment launched its assault on religion, most people still thought that being fully human meant living beyond our solitary selves. Most people still assumed that parents were obliged to children, children were dependent on parents, and that neighborhoods and nations were networks of similar relationships. Meaning and fulfillment are found in identifying such obligations and dependencies and then living in accordance with them.

Today the situation is far different and far more lonesome. We denizens of the modern Western world consider ourselves to be our own independent meaning-makers. Philosophers like Nietzsche have long championed this rise and triumph of the modern autonomous self. But their philosophies have now flowed from the ivory towers into the streets. Nowadays, law, media, entertainment, education, politics, and art all promise us freedom from traditional human limitations. "Follow your heart" is not just a cheesy bumper sticker but the guiding principle of so many real lives.

The call to make our own feelings the ultimate standard of reality has become the cultural air we breathe. Whether we're religious or not, our hearts can be easily seduced by the spell of expressive individualism. But is it an accurate and sustainable vision of what it means to be human? If not, how can we resist it?

We can make a good start by identifying the problem of self-worship and its origins and manifestations in our day. That is where this book by Thaddeus Williams proves so helpful. Williams introduces us to the intellectual architects of the modern notion of human life and how they shape our culture. Thus, Nietzsche and Foucault rub shoulders with Jim Morrison and Marilyn Manson. There are powerful testimonies after each chapter from those who have found liberation from the impossible burden of self-centeredness. Williams thoroughly analyzes, exposes, and debunks the ten commandments of self-worship. Will the problem automatically go away? No. Will all readers be convinced? I hope so. Whatever the outcome, Williams will give you a deeper understanding of the world in which we live and why following God's heart is far better than following your own.

CARL R. TRUEMAN
Grove City College

Introduction

A Misfit's Guide to Sinning Boldly

Oxford's Richard Dawkins, the self-described "militant atheist," opens his dated bestseller *The God Delusion* by laying his cards on the table. He doesn't want you to believe in a god who is "a petty, unjust, unforgiving control-freak."[1] Neither do I. Worship this god and it will make you miserable. It will tear you and the people you care about apart. Just who is this controlling, destructive, malevolent deity? I refer, of course, to the god of self. We all, regardless of our official religious identity, have a tendency, as natural as blinking or breathing, to place ourselves at the center of our own existence. By the end of this book, my prayer is that we would be joyously cured of this "god delusion."

The World's Fastest Growing Religion

"God" is a notoriously slippery word. By "god" I simply mean your most sacred something or someone. A celebrity guru, a romantic partner, a political party, an orgasm, a dopamine hit—each can become our functional deity. It is wherever you look for identity and meaning, whatever you trust as your authoritative truth source, whomever you spend the most energy to please.

There is little doubt who the trending "god" is in my extremely religious home country. Eighty-four percent of Americans believe that the "highest goal of life is to enjoy it as much as possible."[2] Eighty-six percent believe that to be fulfilled requires you to "pursue the things you desire most." Ninety-one percent affirm that "the best way to find yourself is by looking within yourself."

Such self-centeredness is well on its way to achieving world religion status. Over the last century, it has witnessed a global expansion that could give the Christian expansion of the first to fourth centuries and the Muslim expansion of the seventh to eleventh centuries a run for their money. One could make a case that self-worship is the world's fastest growing religion. It is certainly the world's oldest (just read Genesis 3).

In this book, we will meet many of the patron saints of this ancient and trending world religion. Nero turned his self-worship into the enforced faith of an empire. Nietzsche inspired many to become supermen who soar above traditional morality to reach godlike status as sovereign makers of reality. Michel Foucault, Nietzsche's all-star acolyte, took to self-glorification with a twist of sadomasochistic sexuality. Marquis de Sade had done so two centuries before. Jim Morrison of the Doors fame used his baritone crooning and unhinged stage antics to add rock & roll romanticism to Nietzsche's and Sade's dogmas of uninhibited self-assertion.

We will meet Harvard's hippie guru Timothy Leary, who advocated psychedelics as the means to self-exaltation. L. Ron Hubbard added a sci-fi spin to self-deification with his Church of Scientology. The father of modern Satanism, Aleister Crowley, summed up his ethic with the Shakespearean dictum "To thine own self be true." French existentialist Jean-Paul Sartre, beat poet Allen Ginsberg, drag queen RuPaul, tech giant Steve Jobs, and assorted pop divas will join our ensemble of saints. We will see how well the gospel of self-fulfillment panned out for them.

The historic prophets of self-worship are not all remembered by name, studied, and consciously imitated. And not everyone takes it to their extremes. Rather, many now live their daily lives within a more mainstream version of self-worship, slickly advertised for mass consumption.

The Soundtrack of Self-Worship

In addition to saints and prophets, the religion of self is not without its hymns. Ol' Blue Eyes himself, Frank Sinatra, famously sang, "I did it my way," the self-worshipers' classic equivalent to "Amazing Grace." Roxette closes its 1980s pop-rock hit with the looping mantra "Listen to your heart," sung thirteen consecutive times.[3] Country music icon Reba McEntire assures us that "the heart won't lie."[4] Proto-punk rockers The Kinks agree that you should "truly, truly trust your heart."[5] Original bad boys of hard rock Motörhead shout, "Listen to your heart / Listen all your life / Listen to your heart / and then you'll be alright"[6] over gritty power chords.

Then there are the children's songs. In Disney's *Mulan* soundtrack, Stevie Wonder catechizes young, impressionable minds: "You must be true to your heart / That's when the heavens will part.... / Your heart can tell you no lies."[7]

Little feet tap along with an animated swallow named Jacquimo as he serenades Thumbelina: "When you follow your heart, if you have to journey far, / Here's a little trick. You don't need a guiding star. / Trust your ticker, you'll get there quicker."[8]

There are enough tween-targeted self-worship pop songs to fill a year-long playlist. We hear songs about bucking authority, songs about your wildest dreams all coming true, about being a super girl, or some roaring animal goddess who eats people's expectations for breakfast and excretes fireworks and rainbows. Packed auditoriums of adolescents, hands outstretched in worship, have sung in unison with JoJo Siwa: "My life, my rules, my dreams . . . / My life I choose who to be . . . / So I'ma be me . . . / I follow my own lead."[9]

The New Decalogue

The religion of self comes not only with saints and hymns but also with its own sacred commandments. Here are ten:

1. **#liveyourbestlife:** Thou shalt always act in accord with your chief end—to glorify and enjoy yourself forever.
2. **#okboomer:** Thou shalt never be outdated, but always on the edge of the new.
3. **#followyourheart:** Thou shalt obey your emotions at all costs.
4. **#betruetoyourself:** Thou shalt be courageous enough to defy other people's expectations.
5. **#youdoyou:** Thou shalt live your truth and let others live theirs.
6. **#yolo:** Thou shalt pursue the rush of boundary-free experience.
7. **#theanswersarewithin:** Thou shalt trust yourself, never letting anyone oppress you with the antiquated notion of being a "sinner."
8. **#authentic:** Thou shalt invent and advertise thine own identity.
9. **#livethedream:** Thou shalt force the universe to bend to your desires.
10. **#loveislove:** Thou shalt celebrate all lifestyles and love-lives as equally valid.[10]

Of course, many of these hashtags are harmless, perhaps even helpful in certain contexts. A T-ball coach may tell a five-year-old to believe in himself as he sheepishly approaches home plate with a quivering bat. For someone afraid of the big wide world, #yolo may be good advice. Following your dreams and your desires may be sagely wisdom, especially if those dreams and desires arise in the heart of a believer who has yielded to the Holy Spirit. But people often deploy these hashtags with a far more seductive and even diabolical meaning, a meaning that includes false and antibiblical claims about divinity, human nature, sin, salvation, and the future.

With prophets, millions of devotees, a thick hymnal, commandments, and underlying dogmas, self-worship is more profound than a trend or lifestyle choice. It is, in a deep sense, a religion. In countries throughout the Western world, it is arguably the only State-endorsed religion. It would be easy to sneer at self-exaltation as a religion, thinking we have outgrown the fanatical faith of our toddler days. I sneered for years. Then it dawned on me: I wasn't only an outspoken critic of the cult of self, I was and remain a devout member. (Ask those who know me best. I'm practically a saint.) I have been, and will be until the day I die, in one long, painful deconversion process.

Here we reach the liberating and joyous thesis of this book. If you want to become more truly yourself, then break the commandments of self-worship. Break them often. Break them shamelessly. Break them boldly. The subtitle of this book could easily be "The Misfit's Guide to Sinning Boldly against the World's Most Popular Religion" or "How to Be a Twenty-First Century Heretic." I wrote it to convince you to become an atheist about yourself—a defiant, outspoken, strident atheist cured of the delusion of your own deity.

> **If you want to become more truly yourself, then break the commandments of self-worship.**

That is my prayer.

#liveyourbestlife

Thou shalt always act in accord with your chief end—to glorify and enjoy yourself forever.

Glory to Man in the Highest! For Man is the master of things.
—A. C. SWINBURNE, HUMANIST

If a man would make his world large, he must be always making himself small.
—G. K. CHESTERTON, THEIST

What could you do to become as dumb and heartless as a rock? How could you become as plastic and phony as a consumer product? How might you lose your identity and evolve into your significant other's soulless clone? It's simple. Worship your significant other, worship consumer products, or worship a rock.

The Anomaly and Einstein's Law

Poet Ralph Waldo Emerson understood this phenomenon well when he wrote, "A man will worship something—have no doubts about that. . . . Therefore it behooves us to be careful what we worship, for what we are worshiping, we are becoming."[1] Three millennia before Emerson made that connection, the ancient Jewish psalmist had this to say about human-manufactured gods:

> They have mouths, but do not speak;
>   eyes, but do not see.
> They have ears, but do not hear;
>   noses, but do not smell.
> They have hands, but do not feel;
>   feet, but do not walk;
>   and they do not make a sound in their throat.
> Those who make them become like them;
>   so do all who trust in them. (Psalm 115:5–8)

It's true. For better or worse, we become like whatever we worship. Our objects of veneration shape our souls' formation or deformation.

When I wrote a book about this truth several years ago, an anomaly kept popping up in my research.[2] The thesis holds true if we talk about ancient Near Eastern idols. Those who bowed down to chiseled stone deities did have a way of becoming thick and dull like rocks. Emerson's insight that we become what we worship holds true with many gods, except one.

This peculiar idol breaks the rules and defies the data. When you bow before it, you don't become like it at all. You become less and less like it until you are horribly not like it. Unlike all the other gods who make you more like them as you bow, the more you worship your self, the less you become your self. You become a shadow, a specter, an unself. The longer and deeper you stare into the mirror, looking for answers, the more it will feel like looking at Edvard Munch's *The Scream*. This is the strange paradox of self-worship.

Why? It's simple. You were not designed to be the center point of your own psyche. You are not God. Self-deification is a bust. We were never meant to trust in, be defined by, be justified through, be satisfied in, and be captivated by ourselves. We were made to revere Someone infinitely more interesting than ourselves. To speak another modern heresy, it is in a state of self-forgetful reverence that we become most truly and freely ourselves.

This forms the first plank in our case against today's fastest growing religion. The more self-absorbed we are, the less awe we experience; the less awe we experience, the less fully ourselves we become. As Albert

We were made to revere Someone infinitely more interesting than ourselves.

Einstein put it, "A person first starts to live when he can live outside himself."[3] It is awe that is "the source of all true art and all science. He to whom this emotion is a stranger, who can no longer pause to wonder and stand rapt in awe, is as good as dead."[4] The great physicist goes on to locate awe "at the center of true religiousness."[5]

Let us call this Einstein's law: The more you revere something more awesome than yourself, the more alive you become. The more you revere yourself as the most awesome being in existence, the more awful your life becomes.

We are hardwired to function best in a state of awe. This explains why over 35,000 people a year make the inconvenient trek to Mount Everest, 3.5 million to Yosemite, 4.5 million to the Grand Canyon, and 30 million to Niagara Falls.[6] On a gut level, we already know and live Einstein's law. We *want* to be awestruck.

To prove it, let's perform a quick thought experiment. Picture two scenarios. In the first, you lay sprawled on a car hood in the mountains of Tromsø, Norway. Tromsø offers prime viewing of the neon rivers of the aurora borealis. Chartreuse and teal ooze together like watercolor streaks down a black canvas. It is all too awesome (in the original sense of the word of inspiring awe or reverence) to worry about yourself. There you lay, a self-forgetful dust speck with a stellar seat to a celestial light and magic show.

The second scenario also finds you on your back, only this time you are sealed inside your own vintage 1960s sensory deprivation tank. (These were soundproof, lightproof pods filled with salt water, invented in the 1950s and popularized in the 1970s as a way to shut down your senses to allegedly achieve a higher state of consciousness.) As you float in the brine and the blackness, your own consciousness becomes your entire universe. You can analyze yourself endlessly to discover your "true self." My question is this: Where would you feel most truly human, most freely yourself? Take your pick: Tromsø or the tank.

Science Catching Up to Scripture

Two recent scientific findings suggest where I would find you. First is a solid body of research from the social sciences that shows a steep spike in unhappiness over precisely the same time frame that seeking our own happiness first became a celebrated obsession across America. During the 1960s it became trendy and mainstream to interpret the constitutionally protected "pursuit of happiness" in a highly individualistic, subjective, psychological light, as the right, even the entitlement, to make my three best friends—me, myself, and I—happy.

We might think that this trending zeal for happier selves ushered us into a new golden age of freedom and bliss. But the opposite happened. In *The American Paradox*, psychologist David Myers carefully documents how from 1960 to the turn of the twenty-first century, America doubled the divorce rate, tripled the teen suicide rate, quadrupled the violent crime rate, quintupled the prison population, sextupled out-of-wedlock births, and septupled the rate of cohabitation without marriage (which is a significant predictor of eventual divorce).[7] In his work on the neuroscience of happiness, Kevin Corcoran sums up the research bluntly: "It seems the more we desire happiness, pursue it, and consume products we hope will help us to achieve it, the *less* happy and *more* depressed we become."[8]

Social science has gradually caught up with something theologians have been talking about for millennia, "the paradox of hedonism." The more we seek happiness, the more miserable we tend to become. Like gulping saltwater, what seems like a perfectly sane way to quench our thirst for happiness leaves us drinking ourselves into fatal dehydration. In Jesus's words, "Whoever seeks to preserve his life will lose it, but whoever loses his life will keep it" (Luke 17:33).

This leads to a second scientific finding that helps explain the catastrophic rise of misery in our age of self-fulfillment. After exposing his subjects to several "elicitors of awe," University of California, Irvine scientist Paul Piff reported, "We found the same sorts of effects—people felt smaller, less self-important, and behaved in a more prosocial fashion."[9] Piff coined the term "small self" to describe this phenomenon. Awestruck people were more generous, attuned to the needs of others, and caring toward the natural world.

Dr. Shiota of Arizona State University has found that awe also improves our cognition.[10] It makes us less susceptible to bad arguments and more responsive to good ones.[11] There is also a mountain of research from positive psychologists that awe leads to a substantial decline in depression. Want a happier, fuller life? The science is clear: go be awestruck by something bigger than yourself.

Again, the science is gradually catching up with truth that theologians have been trying to tell us for millennia. We are designed to run on awe. Over a hundred times, the Old Testament commands us to express *yirah*—that is, reverence. That reminds me of an unforgettable image from the pen of Robert Jastrow, one of NASA's first and most decorated astronomers. In the last line of his book on twentieth-century breakthroughs in big bang cosmology, Jastrow said that the modern scientist "has scaled the mountain of ignorance; he is about to conquer the highest peak; as he pulls himself over the final rock, he is greeted by a band of theologians who have been sitting there for centuries."[12]

It was once conventional wisdom that the universe has existed forever in a static state. With a little help from Einstein's general theory of relativity, astronomers came to realize that our universe is not eternal after all. It burst into being at a definitive point, and it did so under astonishingly fine-tuned conditions. Jastrow was saying that it took a while, but the science finally caught up with the first line of the Bible—"In the beginning . . ."

What Jastrow described is something like what we see happening to our twenty-first-century understanding of awe. When Jewish theologian Abraham Heschel said, "The greatest insights happen to us in moments of awe," he did not learn that the way Dr. Shiota did.[13] He learned it from the Bible. The church of the first century didn't do longitudinal studies on the "small self." They lived it. Two millennia before Dr. Piff documented "the prosocial effects of awe,"[14] the book of Acts recorded that "awe came upon every soul" (Acts 2:43). In the very next passage, we read that "all who believed were together and had all things in common. And they were selling their possessions and belongings and distributing the proceeds to all, as any had need" (vv. 44–45).[15] How's that for "prosocial effects"?

Theology and science agree—the more awe we experience, the more satisfyingly human we become. We don't just *want* to be awestruck, we *need* to be awestruck. We are made to marvel. It's in our nature. This, again, is why today's fastest growing world religion leaves many people high and dry. Self-worship leaves us aweless and empty because we aren't nearly as awesome as we like to think.

The good news is that there is no scarcity of awesomeness all around us: Those music-making wonders of aeronautical technology we call "birds." The pulsating pixels of a baby's heart on an ultrasound. A Fyodor Dostoevsky novel. A Johann Sebastian Bach or John Williams symphony. A Beatles or Sigur Rós album. A Christopher Nolan or Terrence Malick film. A Michelangelo fresco, Rembrandt woodcut, or Van Gogh canvas. The glistening irises in a lover's eyes. A medium-rare rib eye. An eighteen-year single malt. A kiss. Your next breath. A thunderstorm.

> The more awe we experience, the more satisfyingly human we become.

There are plentiful "elicitors of awe" in our daily worlds. What are they for you? Come up with your top five. Take a moment.

Gods in Our Image

Behold your favorite awe-elicitors long enough and you will find something they all share. None of them are complete unto themselves. None of them are perfect, eternal, or infinite. They have half-lives. They wear off. They lack a certain staying power. Why? Because awe-elicitors exist to signal the reality of something, or rather *Someone*, still more awesome. They are premises, not the conclusion; rivers, not the ocean; sunbeams, not the sun; doorways, not the destination. Consider this book your invitation to follow the ten million signposts of awe in your life to their infinite Source.[16] You become most truly yourself not merely in a state of awe but in a state of awe for the ultimate Source of all that is awesome. And who is that?

It is the God of the Bible. No doubt, that last sentence feels like a record scratch to some of you. A sunset? Oooh! A starlit night? Ahhh! But the God of the Bible pushed by many forms of Christianity? Ughhh! To many, the Christian God hardly seems a worthy object of awe.

As a man who worships the God of the Bible, how do I respond to those who balk at the very idea of Someone I find so thrilling? For me, this is far from hypothetical. I taught History of Atheism at a state college for nearly a decade, with hundreds of atheistic students, many of whom became dear friends (and some who no longer identify as atheists). I have had thousands of hours of vulnerable conversations with people who brazenly reject Christianity. Some never professed faith, and others claim to have deconverted or had a "breakup with God."

A surprising conclusion comes from these conversations. Many renditions of the so-called Christian God shunned by many non-Christians are gods who I, as a Christian, gladly shun too. British theologian A. W. Pink made the point a century ago: "How different is the God of the Bible from the God of modern Christendom! . . . The God of many a present-day pulpit is an object of pity rather than awe-inspiring reverence."[17] Before Pink, Frederick Douglass, the great American abolitionist, recognized "the widest possible difference" between "the Christianity of this land" (which he thought unworthy of the title) and "the Christianity of Christ."[18]

If you find yourself skeptical or positively squeamish about the God of the Bible, it is possible that you reject a counterfeit deity that properly evokes more antipathy than awe.[19] One dear friend rejects a god who allegedly told his cancer-stricken dad to refuse all medical services and to bank on a guaranteed miracle that never came. Another friend rejected a god who denounced her scientific curiosity as the unpardonable sin. Others rejected a god who cared nothing about bringing wholeness and redemption to broken people, only about cold, letter-of-the-law rule enforcement, poised with thunderbolts at the first sight of a moral blunder. These gods share something in common. They trace their origins to the wishful imaginations of bad theologians. Custom-tailoring gods in our own image is a hallmark of bad theology.

Over two and a half millennia ago, a Greek philosopher called Xenophanes saw the problem. "Men believe that the gods are clothed and shaped and speak like themselves," Xenophanes observed.

Custom-tailoring gods in our own image is a hallmark of bad theology.

"If oxen and horses and lions could draw and paint they would delineate their gods in their own image.... The Thracians [believe] that their gods have blue eyes and red hair."[20] In the eighteenth century, Voltaire put it memorably: "If God made us in his image, we have certainly returned the compliment."[21]

Xenophanes and Voltaire were on to something. Most forms of theism are self-worship incognito, our individual personalities and prejudices disguised as something transcendent and sacred. The moralistic whistleblower projects his cosmic guilt-tripper into the sky. There is a prosperity-showering deity for the materialist, a lifeless X at the end of a neat logical syllogism for the philosopher, a neo-Nazi god for the white nationalist, a Marxist god for the hard leftist.

Each of these manufactured gods has been marketed as the Christian God. So when I say my goal is to convince you to become an atheist about the god of self, that includes the gods of other selves. It certainly includes "Christian" gods conjured up by other imperfect people.[22] To skeptics, I say bluntly that you have likely rejected some overblown projection of an unholy jerk. If so, then I am right there with you.

While rejecting the deities of his day, Xenophanes carved out an important distinction. He believed that, despite all our anthropomorphic gods, "one God" still exists and "in neither his form or his thought is he like unto mortals."[23] Centuries before Xenophanes, the Bible put it starkly: "God is not man" (Num. 23:19). Calling the idols of his age "false," "worthless," and "a work of delusion," and after comparing man-made gods to "scarecrows in a cucumber field" (apparently quite a zinger in the ancient Near East), Jeremiah went on to acknowledge, "There is none like you, O LORD" (Jer. 10:5–6, 14–15). God faults the Israelites, saying, "You thought that I was one like yourself" (Ps. 50:21). But "My thoughts are not your thoughts, neither are your ways my ways, declares the LORD" (Isa. 55:8).

So, dear reader, I ask you keep an open mind to the possibility that, for all your proper unbelief, there exists a Being far worthier of awe and enjoyment than anyone you have ever imagined. There is a God to be discovered, not invented; a living Person, not a projection; a Being who defies and exceeds our expectations. Crack open the door to belief, just a sliver. You just may find someone there— Someone awesome, uncreated, and unimaginably good.

Two Hymns

I have sketched a case that given our shortage of awesomeness, putting ourselves at the center of the universe strips us of awe and renders us deeply unhappy. But God is awesome in all the ways the deepest recesses of our souls long to be awestruck. Here are fourteen ways that God is a far more excellent object of awe than the images we see in the mirror:

1. God never lies or breaks promises. We do.
2. God is not bound by time, but sees it all—past, present, and future—with perfect clarity. He was here long before us, even before time existed, which is one of his ideas. We are stuck in this moment, hazy about much of the past and oblivious to much of the future.
3. God is self-existent, requiring no one to bring him into being or keep him alive. We needed a mother and a father to bring us into existence. We need oxygen, food, water, and (for some of you) caffeine to continue existing.
4. God is sovereign, enthroned over the entire universe; Lord over galaxies, nations, and subatomic particles. We might pretend to be sovereign, but our control over the world is a pipe dream.
5. God is not bound by space; he is present everywhere. We are where we are right now, circumscribable. We could draw ten-foot circles around one another and say truly, "This circle contains you."
6. God is infinitely satisfying. Our best attempts to be the source of ultimate satisfaction for others will leave us all exhausted, jaded, and disillusioned.
7. God is the supreme Artist who thought up glowing space nebulae, Technicolor sunsets, the flavor of watermelon and coffee beans, the melodies of songbirds, the kaleidoscopic patterns in a human iris, and everything else beautiful in creation. We are created to be creative like him, but for all our most sublime artistic feats, he is the true Master.

8. God can create *ex nihilo* by an act of sheer artistic will-power. We can create only from pre-existing stuff.

9. God is gracious and merciful, bestowing ill-deserved favor on his creatures. We can be petty, grudge-harboring, and spiteful. We need grace to draw our next breaths.

10. God knows all things and his wisdom is boundless. He can never learn, be surprised, or fit fully into the boxes of finite minds. For us, the universe is full of question marks, and the more we know the more we realize we don't know.

11. God is one Being who exists eternally as three equal and inter-loving Persons—the Father, the Son, and the Holy Spirit. As such, God has always been engaged in interpersonal loving community in his very Being, and he invites you into that love. Our love as humans can be beautiful and authentic but it pales in comparison to the infinite love we are offered in the triune God.

12. God feels perfectly. He is never temperamental, moody, or overcome by wild emotions. Our emotions often vacillate and fall out of sync with reality.

13. God is holy, transcending all sin, evil, and injustice. We slip into sin more times a day than we can count.

14. God is infinitely and altogether awesome. We are not.

Having seen something of the Creator-creature distinction, the difference between God and us, let us close with two hymns. In 1879 British philosopher W. K. Clifford wrote,

> The dim and shadowy outline of the superhuman deity fades slowly away from us.... We perceive with greater and greater clearness the shape of a yet grander and nobler figure. . . . Our father Man [note well the capital M] looks out upon us with the fire of eternal youth in his eyes, and says, "before Jehovah was, I am."[24]

The longer and louder we sing the praises of man, the less awe-struck we become. We buckle under the weight of our own infinite expectations on ourselves. If we want to inhale true freedom, then let us join with saints around the globe in the words of a classic hymn composed shortly after Clifford wrote his sacrilegious hymn to human greatness:

> Oh Lord, my God
> When I, in awesome wonder
> Consider all the worlds Thy hands have made
> I see the stars, I hear the rolling thunder
> Thy power throughout the universe displayed

[I happen to be typing these words on a balcony under the stars as the Mexican sky lights up and thunder rolls. Awe inspiring!]

> Then sings my soul, my Savior God to Thee
> How great Thou art, how great Thou art
> Then sings my soul, my Savior God to Thee
> How great Thou art, how great Thou art.[25]

A Heretic's Testimonial

Joni Eareckson Tada is an author, a speaker, and an international advocate for people with disabilities. Her ministry, Joni and Friends (http://www.joniandfriends.org), provides programs to special needs families, as well as training to churches worldwide. She is also a heretic against the cult of self-worship. She boldly breaks the #liveyourbestlife commandment. This is her story.

Lately, I've been whispering the question David asked in 1 Chronicles 17:16: "Who am I, O Lord God, and what is my house, that you have brought me thus far?" *Who am I to enjoy a platform on national radio for forty years? Who am I that I should be so blessed in marriage to Ken for forty years? And how did I ever have the strength to survive fifty-five years as a quadriplegic in a wheelchair?*

The truth is, I don't have the strength. I still wake up every morning needing God desperately. Like David, I often confess, "I am poor and needy" (Ps. 40:17). Perhaps that's how God brought me this far. I can't say, but I do know that "the eyes of the Lord range throughout the earth to strengthen those whose hearts are fully committed to him" (2 Chron. 16:9 NIV). God is searching high and low for weak people who love him so that he can pour into them *his* strength. Maybe that's my story, but how I arrived here is not for me to say. I just keep praising my sovereign God with every milestone I pass.

It's the noble cause of Christ to which I've dedicated myself for decades, and I can't think of anything that gives me more joy. Yet as I reach the milestone of fifty-five years of quadriplegia—not to mention two bouts of cancer, severe breathing issues, COVID-19, and chronic pain—I hold tightly to Acts 20:24 (NIV): "I consider my life worth nothing to me; my only aim is to finish the race and complete the task the Lord Jesus has given me—the task of testifying to the good news of God's grace."

When a broken neck upended my life all those years ago, I was depressed and devastated. God transformed my heart, changed my attitude, and showed me there are more important things in life than walking. Aging with quad-riplegia may be filled with extra challenges, but it doesn't demoralize me. With God's help, I hold everything lightly. I try not to grasp at my fragile life, nor coddle it or minimize my activities at Joni and Friends just because I'm getting older, growing weaker, and dealing with more pain. Rather, I find great comfort and joy in dying to self and living every day to serve the Lord Jesus and others around the world whose disabilities are far more profound than mine.

What else could be more important than practicing Christianity, with sleeves rolled up, among the needy? When I do become tired, I'm inspired by the life of Jesus, who, even as he was nailed on his cross and in great pain, nevertheless kept serving others (like the thief, his mother, and the soldiers who needed forgiveness). Ephesians 5:1 tells me to imitate him. So I'm heaven bent on honoring my Jesus, serving others, finishing the race, and complet-ing the task of testifying to gospel grace. So here I sit, glad that I have not been healed on the outside, but glad that I have been healed on the inside—healed from my own self-centered wants and wishes.

—Joni

A Heretic's Prayer

God,
You are true to your promises, self-existent, sovereign,
unbound by space and time, infinitely satisfying, the
source of beauty, full of grace and mercy, all-knowing

and incomprehensible, all-loving and triune, changelessly perfect, holy, and awesome in every way our souls long to be awestruck. We are none of those things. Lord, help our dull hearts better align with reality. Help us feel more and more awe at your supreme awesomeness. Amen.

A Heretic's Field Manual

Before moving on to the next chapter, do three or four of the following to sharpen your skills at violating the commandment to #liveyourbestlife:

1. Get out in God's creation. Stop to observe and soak in the creative genius manifest around you. Thank him for it.
2. Sing a hymn. Old hymns like "How Great Thou Art," "Fairest Lord Jesus," "Holy, Holy, Holy," "Come Thou Fount of Every Blessing," and "Be Thou My Vision" break us out of self-centeredness and recalibrate our emotions to be awestruck at the size and splendor of God. Make a playlist and let these old God-centered songs be the soundtrack to your day.
3. Turn off your devices, eliminate distractions, and slowly read through Isaiah 46. As you read, thank God for each aspect of his awesomeness you see revealed in the text.
4. Attend a gathering of people who worship God. Join in the songs, no matter your vocal skill (or lack thereof). Don't sing with a self-centered expectation of receiving a spiritual buzz, but purely to melodically declare truth about God to God in unison with others. As C. S. Lewis said, "The

perfect church service would be one we were almost un-aware of. Our attention would have been on God."[26]

5. Set aside five minutes to pray through the twelve divine attributes in the previous prayer. Don't pray about your-self and your needs at all for this particular prayer. In-stead, simply thank God for being who he is. Ask him to help you be increasingly awestruck by his manifold glo-ries. If helpful, use the following acrostic about the God at the BIBLE'S CENTER to help guide your prayer:

The God at the **BIBLE'S CENTER** is . . .

> **Biblically revealed:** God is knowable because he has made himself knowable, communicating who he is by inspiring sixty-six books of the Bible. Read Num-bers 23:19, 2 Timothy 3:16–17, and 2 Peter 1:21.
>
> **I Am / self-existent:** God exists objectively and not as a subjective human projection. He *is*. God is also self-existent, requiring no one and nothing to bring him into existence. Read Exodus 3:14, Psalm 90:2, and Acts 17:24.
>
> **Beyond time:** God is not bound by time, but creates it, sees it all with equal clarity, and acts within it. He does not progress or change over time, and as a perfect being, he does not need to. Read Psalm 102:25–27, Isaiah 46:9–10, and Revelation 1:8.
>
> **Lord of everything:** God, as a sovereign being, al-ways does whatever he pleases, however he pleases, whenever he pleases, to whomever or whatever he

pleases for the sake of his glory. Read Daniel 4:34–35, Isaiah 46:8–10, and Ephesians 1:11.

Everywhere: God, as creator of space, is not space itself nor limited by it. As an omnipresent being, God may hide, but there is no hiding from him. Read 2 Chronicles 6:18, Psalm 139:7–10, and Jeremiah 23:23–24.

Satisfying: God is the supreme object of deepest joy possible, the only infinite source of all true, lasting human fulfillment, and the chief purpose for our existence. Read Psalm 63:1–5, Ecclesiastes 1:14, and John 10:10.

Creative: God, as creator of everything from Scripture to sunsets, is the supreme artist and architect. He is the ultimate source of all true beauty and order in the universe. Read Genesis 1:1–31, Job 38–39, and Hebrews 1:1–3, 10–12.

Emotional: God feels genuine grief at his creatures' rebellion, anger at their trivialization of his glory, jealousy at their worship of false gods, and joy at their salvation and obedience. Read Genesis 6:6, Isaiah 1:11–14, and Zephaniah 3:17.

Needy-saving: God, as a gracious and merciful being, saves those who cannot save themselves, forgives sin, and lavishes utterly undeserved favor on his creatures. Read Ezekiel 16, Romans 3:24, and Ephesians 1:3–2:18.

Thinking: God is all-knowing, the source of all truth who can neither learn nor be surprised. As a being of infinite intellect, he is not fully comprehensible to finite human minds. Read Isaiah 55:8–9, Psalm 139:1–4, and Romans 11:33.

Engaged in love: God is one being who exists as three coequal, coeternal, and interloving persons—the Father, Son, and Holy Spirit. This triune God is love and profoundly loves his creatures. Read Isaiah 43:10, Luke 3:21–22, and John 17:20–28.

Righteous / holy: God is the source and standard of all goodness. As a holy, holy, holy being, he exists in unique moral splendor, separate from all sin and corruption, which he justly punishes. Read Deuteronomy 32:1–4, Isaiah 6:1–4, and 1 Peter 1:16.

#okboomer

Thou shalt never be outdated, but always on the edge of the new.

Satanism is about worshiping yourself because you are responsible for your own good and evil.

—MARILYN MANSON, ROCK STAR

Ever since the Garden of Eden, [self-deification] has been the first and most fundamental of human sins. Satan did not tempt Adam and Eve to worship him but to worship themselves—their own freedom, their rights, their potential for becoming gods.

—PAUL HIEBERT, ANTHROPOLOGIST

How many advertisements do you think reach the eyes and ears of the average American every twenty-four hours? One hundred? One thousand? In the late 1990s researchers approximated the number around sixteen thousand![1] That factors to nearly six million ads a year. That was in the late 1990s, before the worldwide explosion of social media and the smart phone revolution. Now you can hardly check in on your friends or play a round of solitaire without being bombarded by magical supplements that give you an Olympian body without the inconvenience of exercise.

A great many of the marketing teams and media influencers who determine much of what you look at on a daily basis ply their wares by advertising self-worship as something innovative, edgy, and forward-thinking. We are conditioned to look down our noses at the traditional and conventional. This contempt for the past is often captured with hashtags like #okboomer, writing off older generations' perspectives as out of touch and irrelevant, and, more recently, #cheugy (pronounced "chew-gee"), a Gen-Z term popular on TikTok, coined by a woman in her twenties named Gaby Rasson to describe anything uncool, untrendy, and old. The truth is that self-worship is as #cheugy as it gets. It represents the most ancient and worn-out ideology known to humanity. We can't subscribe to it without becoming regressive ubertraditionalists.

Origins

To see just how backward-thinking self-worship is, look at humanity's origin story recorded in the book of Genesis. First, a quick word about origins. We are obsessed with origins. We flock to big-budget origin stories of our favorite superheroes. We enlist 23andMe or Ancestry to discover the origins of our families and genetic codes. Most adopted children seek out their birth parents at some point. We fill our social media feeds with ultrasound photos, first-step, first-word, and first-soccer-goal videos, carefully documenting the origins of our offspring. We frequent therapists' couches to understand the origins of our anxieties. Astrophysicists ponder big bang cosmology. Anthropologists and archaeologists scavenge the globe to unearth the birth of civilizations. Why all the fuss about where things came from? The short answer is because it matters how things begin. It really does. You are better able to understand and enjoy something when you know its origin.

Another word for origin is "genesis." The opening book of the Bible tells us not only about the origin of the universe, stars, oceans, amoebas, blue whales, cheetahs, watermelons, carnations, and hummingbirds. It also tells *our* origin story as human beings, and, therefore, sheds light on who we are now. Abraham Kuyper noted, "The origins of all that still stirs your interest, of all that surrounds you in your personal life, and of all that goes on within your heart, are unfolded before us in the book of Genesis."[2]

One particularly bewildering detail in humanity's origin story carries massive insight for understanding ourselves today. In the garden in Genesis 3, we behold the Tree of Knowledge of Good and Evil alongside Adam and Eve. Note well the words the serpent uses to tempt humanity's first couple. Eating from the forbidden fruit would make Adam and Eve "like God, knowing good and evil" (Gen. 3:5). How does God know good and evil?[3] That is no small question. It is a key to unlocking not only the whole mystery of the Genesis story but also the most pressing problems of life in the twenty-first century, and indeed your own quest to find yourself.

Knowing as Making

We typically use the English word "know" in ways that blur the meaning of Genesis. Allow me to offer a real-life scenario in which our English word "know" comes closer to the ancient Hebrew of Genesis 3. After college I lived in a bachelor pad with friends. One of those friends, Dave, was a founding member of a band called Linkin Park. Their debut album *Hybrid Theory* had recently gone multiplatinum. (It was surreal seeing Grammys on the mantle in what was an otherwise dumpy apartment.) Dave, or "Phoenix" as he is known to fans, was hard at work with his bandmates crafting their sophomore release, *Meteora*, which went on to be certified platinum seven times over. Dave would return from the studio daily, and we would listen through the rough concept tracks of what became over fifty songs, only twelve of which survived the final cut.

I had questions. What effect are you using there? What inspired that track? How did you make that part sound so face-meltingly huge? I never once stumped him. Dave *knew* the songs. He did not know them because he had blasted them on the radio over and over or studied the sheet music bar by bar. He knew them because he *made* them. Dave knew why the song was that way—because he personally chose to make it that way. He had knowledge of his music that the rock critics and die-hard fans could never attain. He had a *maker's knowledge*, the very power offered in Genesis 3.

Knowing something because you made it is the kind of knowledge that God has of his universe. He knows it because he personally chose it to be what it is.[4] God *knowing* good and evil, then, is Hebrew shorthand for God creating, composing, determining, and defining what is good and evil.

The Beatles and Creed

We tend to hear "good and evil" as moral words. This does not
jibe with the ancient Hebrew of Genesis 3. We have just seen that
"knowing" here means knowing by making something yourself,
and God does not directly make evil. "His work is perfect, for all
his ways are justice" (Deut. 32:4). Instead, we should read "good
and evil" as a Hebrew idiom. It is an ancient Jewish way of speaking that names polar opposites to include everything in between.
It would be like saying "black and white" to refer to every color, or
"the Beatles and Creed" to refer to every rock band. "Good and evil"
is Hebrew shorthand for *everything*.[5]

When we decode the ancient Hebrew, we see that God, as God,
defines the meaning of everything. He "made all things" (Isa. 44:24).
He "laid the foundation of the earth" and "determined its meas-
urements" (Job 38:4–5). He knows "the ordinances of the heavens"
and established "their rule on the earth" (Job 38:33). God is the
originator, the determiner, the authority, the boundary-setter, the
ultimate meaning-maker of the entire universe. All of this liberating truth is compacted into that tiny Hebrew
phrase translated "knowing good and evil."

God defines the meaning of everything.

What, then, was the tree? It was the truth
expressed in wood and chlorophyll—that God
is God, the supreme knowing maker of the universe, and we are
not. He is the Creator; we are the created. The tree was a landmark
to the Creator-creature distinction. It said to Adam and Eve, "You
are not the ultimate standard of what is true, good, and beautiful."
The command to not eat its fruit was a command to live authentically before the godhood of God and our own not-God-ness.

The clever serpent insinuated to Eve that God's hidden motive
in forbidding the fruit was fear: God is threatened by human

potential. He trembles like an insecure junior higher at the thought of others showing him up. He wants to keep his creatures dumb and docile to protect his oh-so-fragile ego. This, of course, was a lie. Satan projected his own insecurities into the sky. God had granted his first image-bearers an astounding amount of creative power. He called them to be poets, naming the animals. He commanded them to be culture-makers who mirror their Creator by multiplying the net beauty in the universe.

Baked into the serpent's lie was the falsehood that power is a zero-sum game. Nietzsche and his ideological offspring echoed this lie millennia later. In Nietzsche's words, "This world is firm, iron magnitude of force that does not grow bigger or smaller, that does not expend itself but only transforms itself . . . increasing here and at the same time decreasing there."[6] In other words, since power is a fixed constant, the only way to gain, say, one hundred units of power would be to take one hundred power-units from others.

This is a false and sinister assumption. Power is not a zero-sum game. If you've ever had a good parent, a good boss, a good teacher, or studied the meaning of Jesus washing feet and enduring the cross,[7] you know that empowering others does not rob us of power; it makes us more truly powerful. If you've ever been on a power trip, lording power over others, or studied the fate of tyrants like Nero, Hitler, Mussolini, and Saddam Hussein, you know that stripping others of power is the path to becoming pathetic and powerless.

The serpent deceived Adam and Eve with this bogus assumption about zero-sum power. "God wants to retain absolute power, so he must keep you utterly powerless. Pay no mind to the vast orchards around you—you know, the ones God made you stewards over, teeming with beauty and possibility and life-giving deliciousness ripe for the picking. No. Look at *this* tree and this tree *only*, with its forbidden fruit. If you want real power, you have to stop *bowing* to God and instead *become* god. This fruit is your ticket to that supremacy. Eat it. Take a dose of divine power for yourselves. Taste sweet liberation from your cosmic oppressor. *Vive la révolution* against the hegemonic power of heaven!"

Every temptation is some version of that lie. Listen closely and you can still hear the old serpent hiss, "Why settle for being lowly creatures when you can be almighty creators? Believe in yourssselves."[8] What the serpent advertised as the fruit of freedom turned out to be the bitter pill of bondage. Evil always delivers the opposite of what it promises. False advertising abounds. "Follow your heart. . . . If it's in your heart, go for it. Don't listen to other people,"[9] says comedian Maz Jobrani. "Break the rules, stand apart, ignore your head, and follow your heart,"[10] says pop diva Paula Abdul. Blended Scotch is for "heart followers only," as a recent ad tells you to "follow your heart with Cutty Sark."[11] A Minecraft ad invites kids to "Create Your World."[12] It's the same deception but with stickier slogans and a paper-thin veneer of glamour. As Jeremy Rifkin puts it, "It is our creation now. We make the rules. We establish the parameters of reality. We create the world, and because we do, we no longer feel beholden to outside forces. We no longer have to justify our behavior, for we are now the architects of the universe. We are responsible for nothing outside ourselves, for we are the kingdom, the power, and the glory forever and ever."[13] Like Adam and Eve, we follow the old lie that we are ultimate Creators rather than image-bearing creatures to our demise.

> The fruit of freedom turned out to be the bitter pill of bondage.

The New Puritans

We have seen that attempting to create your own reality is hardly as cutting edge, rebellious, or unconventional as it seems. It is embarrassingly old. True heretics reject humanity's oldest lie. They refuse to be traditionalists. They use their God-given intellects to multiply the beauty and life in the world without the delusion that they are supreme.[14] They take the lesson of the tree that God is God and they are not. Their feet are firmly grounded in the deep reality of the Creator-creature distinction. They reason, learn, and innovate with humility. They take God's words more seriously than they take the shifty whims of their own finite emotions. In short, true heretics refuse to live their lives by the tired, failed, retrograde dogmas of an old serpent.

It follows from this that our perceptions could use a good recalibration. Picture Jim Morrison with his disheveled brown locks and leather pants, the charismatic baritone vocalist of the psychedelic rock group the Doors. He was a major Nietzsche enthusiast, the self-appointed "Lizard King," famous (or infamous) for gyrating and exposing himself on stage, spewing obscenities at crowds, a bohemian lifestyle marked by cryptic, dark poetry, sleeping with anonymous groupies, and imbibing copious amounts of booze, LSD, and heroin. Many people memorialize Morrison as a kind of visionary lothario, untamable, courageously pointing us toward a higher state of consciousness by dropping his trousers and defiling tradition. The truth is, in light of Genesis 3, we may as well think of Morrison as an uptight church lady with an imposing perm. His strict obedience to the millennia-old code of a preachy snake made him an ubertraditionalist.

There was also French intellectual Michel Foucault with his trademark shaved head and mock turtlenecks. With his postmodern philosophy and sadomasochistic sexual exploration, he took to the old dogmas of self-worship with puritanical zeal. He might as well have sported a buckled black pilgrim hat and a white butterfly collar.

Or take the celebrated drag queen RuPaul. As he put it in an interview with *Time*, "Drag has always served a purpose. We mock identity. We're shape-shifters. We are God in drag. And that's our role to remind people of that."[15] Hmm. The promise of becoming gods who can shape-shift and create new identities by our own willpower? That's so 6000 BC or 6 million BC, depending on your cosmology. Either way, it's hardly cutting edge.

The self-inventing innovators of our age are so traditional they make boomers look avant-garde. Self-worship perpetuates what is literally the oldest lie. It's hypertraditional, hyperfundamentalist, #Cheugy with a capital *C*.

At the 2023 Grammys, pop icon Madonna took the stage holding a dominatrix riding crop and expressing, "Thanks to all the rebels out there forging a new path." She then introduced Sam Smith and Kim Petras's performance of a song entitled "Unholy."

Many were shocked by Smith and Petras's performance, replete with demonic imagery. This was hardly innovative. In 2021 the Lil Nas X released his 666 shoes featuring a pentagram and drop of human blood, and a music video in which he gives Satan a lap dance. In 2022 Demi Lovato released her *Holy Fvck* album, in which she sings that she is "Like a serpent in the garden," "the fruit that was forbidden / I don't keep my evil hidden . . . / I'm the sexorcist."

Satanic themes have long been a fixture of American music, going back, at least, to legends of Robert Johnson trading his soul to the devil. AC/DC released "Highway to Hell" in 1979. Van Halen released "Runnin' with the Devil" in 1978. The Rolling Stones released "Sympathy for the Devil" in 1968. *This Is Spinal Tap* was hilariously mocking all of this back as far back as 1984. As Thomas More observed five centuries ago, "The devil, that proud spirit, cannot endure to be mocked." Perhaps we who recognize Christ's victory over darkness could do with more mockery and less doomsday forecasting when faced with blatant displays of the demonic.

Jesus already put Satan and his minions to cosmic shame by his work on the cross (Col. 2:15).

After the performance, Petras stated, "I just hope that it inspires kids at home." What precisely was supposed to inspire kids at home? Smith, donning devil horns, received choreographed worship, while Petras, legs spread, gyrated inside a cage in the face of multiple strippers. How inspiring for the kids.

What was the driving message of Smith and Petras, two biological males with XY chromosomes, the first who identifies as gender fluid and the second who has undergone gender mutilation (at the age of sixteen) to identify as a female? Their predictable mainstream message is that our desires define reality and we should live our own truths. This was precisely the message of Anton LaVey, the founder of the actual Church of Satan. LaVey used Satan as a metaphor for bold obedience to one's own desires over and against all traditions and social expectations. In that sense, the "Unholy" performance was indeed satanic.

But there is a deeper sense, as we have seen, the biblical sense. The message of self-exaltation is hardly, in Madonna's words, "forging a new path." It merely repeats the ancient temptation of Satan, the offer to become "like God, knowing good and evil" (Gen. 3:5). Smith and Petras overhype what is literally the oldest lie in human history. Their edginess is archaic, their innovation hopelessly outdated.

Kim Petras was asked about the personal inspiration behind the performance. Petras replied, "I personally grew up wondering about religion and wanting to be part of it, but slowly realizing it doesn't want me to be a part of it." To Kim and all those who have felt rejected by the church and embraced the message of self-exaltation, I offer the following words in love:

Your rejection of religion hasn't made you nonreligious. You are still bowing, only to the finite creation rather than the infinite

Creator. Let me be crystal clear: You are loved in a way that no sexual experience can grant. We absolutely want you to be a part of Jesus's movement to bring healing and redemption to a fallen cosmos. We, like you, have made spectacles of our self-worship. But there is grace for us all. Jesus is infinitely more joyous and meaningful than all the world's accolades and affirmation. He is where our deepest identity is found. Ever since Jesus's death and resurrection, everything changed. The system of self-glorification is on its way out. Please, don't find yourself on the wrong side of the future. Don't spend your career parroting the doomed dogmas of an ancient snake. Repent. Find eternal life in Jesus.

The Wrong Side of the Future

Today's avant-garde are outdated in a still more profound sense. They are on the wrong side of the future. Let me explain. In a passage theologians call the *protoevangelium* (first gospel), God promised someone who would reverse the devastating effects of humanity's self-worship. He promised a serpent-crusher (Gen. 3:15). Falling for the serpent's offer to be sovereign gods unto themselves, Adam and Eve plunged the universe and their offspring into an age of death and decay. As an old headline from the Christian satire site *The Babylon Bee* put it, "Couple Follows Their Hearts; Billions Dead." Scripture calls this age of death, toil, warfare, doom, injustice, and heartbreak the *ha-olam hazeh* in Hebrew, or "the present age." Everything in your newsfeed that boils your blood, saps your joy, or exhausts your soul—these are the marks of the present age. (We have barely begun to reckon with the psychological and spiritual toll of our smart devices and social media broadcasting the tragedies of the present age into our consciousness faster and in far greater volume than any time in human history.)

The serpent of Genesis 3 has become "the god of this world"

(2 Cor. 4:4), "the ruler of this world" (John 14:30; 1 John 5:19), and "the prince of the power of the air" (Eph. 2:2). To expand his dark kingdom (Matt. 12:26), the serpent deceives, infects, accuses, harasses, blinds, shackles, steals, murders, and devours human beings (John 8:44; 10:10; 2 Cor. 4:4; 1 Peter 5:8). How does he carry out his hell-bent mission? He repeats the same lie he used to con Adam and Eve. He makes each new generation and every individual the same bogus promise that we can be sovereign unto ourselves. He promises us autonomy to advance his nefarious agenda because he knows that the extent to which we assert our self-rule is the extent to which we unwittingly swear allegiance to his dark kingdom. Self-worship is mere service to the serpent, disguised as freedom.

By dying and rising back to life, Jesus stomped the old serpent's skull and launched *ho-olam ha-ba*—"The age to come." What is the age to come? It is the breaking in of the kingdom of God over and against Satan's kingdom—the age of *shalom*, undiminishing joy, love, and peace—the happy ending all great stories point toward, great choreography stretches for, great poetry aches for, and bad art mocks. We get fleeting scents of it with our faces pressed in a magnolia flower. We get tantalizing appetizers in a skillfully crafted meal. We glimpse it in a Pacific sunset after a fire. We sense it in a warm embrace from a loved one. We get audio samples of the age to come in deep mirth and laughter among friends or in a congregation swept up together in melodic worship. "The age to come" is what Jesus started when he rose and what he will consummate when he returns.

Are we living in *ha-olam hazeh* or *ho-olam ha-ba*? Yes is the Bible's answer. We live in the shaded area of a Venn diagram in which the circles of "the present age" and "the age to come" overlap, simultaneously, strategically competing for our minds, squared off in moment-by-moment warfare of eternal, cosmic proportions. Every day, ten thousand times a day, we choose which age we prefer, which kingdom and, therefore, which royal lord we swear allegiance to—Jesus, "the blessed and only Sovereign, the King of kings and Lord of lords" (1 Tim. 6:15), or "the prince of the power of the air."

Only one of these two kingdoms has a future. The other is on its way out, crawling like a fatally wounded insurgent toward oblivion. By dying and walking out of the grave, Jesus broke the rules of the present age (Gal. 1:4), guaranteeing its final demise. He dealt a death blow to death itself. Decay and destruction no longer have the final word. His cross and empty tomb guarantee that truth, goodness, beauty, and justice prevail. Jesus wins, the serpent loses.

Decay and destruction no longer have the final word.

It follows that the serpent's lie of self-worship loses. When we bow to ourselves, when we are self- rather than Christ-centered, we are on the wrong side of the future, taking sides with a crushed serpent who is doomed to sulfur and destruction. But when we bow to the reality of Christ's reign as King, we step into his winning kingdom, the forward-flow and glorious destiny of the cosmos. By worshiping him rather than ourselves, we find ourselves on the right side of the future.

A Heretic's Testimonial

Oscar Navarro serves as senior vice president of Living Waters and cohosts the *Way of the Master!* show and podcast. **Kelli Navarro** works in the fields of mental health and special education. They are also heretics against the cult of self-worship. They boldly break the #okboomer command. This is their story.

(Oscar) grew up in a fatherless home. I was told he was a drinker, a fighter, and was himself fatherless. Having been born to a teenage mom struggling with addiction made my early years wrought with uncertainty. I'd had three step-fathers by the time I was thirteen. One was sexually abusive, and another was verbally and physically abusive. I spent seven years as a young boy in the hands of a sexual predator whose access to me was unbridled. He was replaced by a man who tormented my mom, siblings, and me with physical and verbal dominance. After I called the police on husband number two, my mom kicked me out of the house. I was thirteen.

I got kicked out of three junior high schools, twice for fighting. During high school I lived in my grandma's one-bedroom condo, sleeping on her couch. But she kicked me out after my sophomore year of high school. I was on my own. These stories normally end with the kid on the streets, addicted to drugs. But I was determined to make something of myself. I found financial success early with a thriving career. Following my heart and trying to be my own god turned me to atheism and material wealth. Religion seemed a bore and something only the weak needed—as Karl Marx put it, an "opiate for the masses." I didn't need it. I was, in my own foolish eyes, too wise, strong, and independent to lean on such a crutch. Plus, the thought of worshiping a supreme being interfered with my self-supremacy.

From the outside it looked like I was doing okay, but a closer look and you would have seen an insecure, angry, and socially destructive person. I thought I could create a new legacy with financial freedom, but I dragged all the sin and pain from my childhood into adulthood.

But God saved me. The Holy Spirit softened my heart to the gracious love and healing power of Jesus. I am now married with three wonderful children. Every time my wife and I sit down for prayers and devotional time with our kids, I am reminded of the redeeming work of God. Instead of following in my fatherless father's footsteps, my three children have a dad who can point them to their one true Father in heaven. The "old, boring, and dying" faith was where I learned just how freeing it is that God is God and I am not.

Twelve years ago, I (Kelli) was lost, broken, and helpless. Psalm 40:2 says, "He brought me up from a desolate pit, out of the muddy clay, and set my feet on a rock, making my steps secure" (CSB). As a single mother, I was in a deep, muddy pit and desperately needed a rock to stand on. Sustaining my whole identity myself, even just surviving, felt like a crushing weight. Little did I know I was being pursued by the only One who could truly define me. The Holy Spirit snapped me out of my isolated trance just long enough to realize I needed to make serious, life-changing decisions.

Back then I would have told you I believed in God, but that was the extent of it. The few outspoken Christians I knew seemed so judgmental. I was intrigued by what church had to offer but wanted no part of feeling shamed by others as a single mom. But God doesn't wait for us to get our act together to save us. We can never save ourselves, but his grace can. The Lord surrounded me with amazing friends who encouraged, supported, and prayed, one of which was my now husband, Oscar. My security is not found in my ability to be a spiritual superstar, an amazing wife, or a "do-it-all" mother. I've tried those out, and, spoiler alert, it isn't pretty. My identity is not found in my past trauma, although God uses that too. My identity is anchored in the deep and pure love of God. His grace is sufficient no matter your past, present, or future. Walking with Christ does not guarantee a "rainbows and unicorns" life, but it guarantees something far better, Christ himself, in all his kindness and beauty. Don't be so burdened with the impossible weight of self. Jesus will bear your burdens. Come to him.

—Oscar and Kelli

A Heretic's Prayer

God,

You are the Creator, we are the created. You are the sovereign meaning-maker. You define reality. You made us in your image to wield tremendous creative power for your glory, for our flourishing, and for the good of the cosmos. But, like Adam and Eve, we have fallen for the old lie that we can erase the Creator-creature distinction and claim the scepter and crown for ourselves, that we can reign as sovereign lords, play by our own rules, become ultimate meaning-makers of the universe. By pretending to be you, by listening to an ancient snake, we have brought lies, injustice, and ugliness where we should have brought the true, the good, and the beautiful. Please forgive us for our self-destructive and futile rebellion against the fundamental structure of reality. Help us to live authentically before the truth that you are God and we are not. Amen.

A Heretic's Field Manual

Before moving on to the next chapter, do at least three of the following to sharpen your skills at violating the #okboomer commandment:

1. Take a walk in nature. Note how the intricate beauty and design around you was not thought up by you. Let the Creator-creature distinction settle into your heart as you stroll along and ponder how much God has made without your help and how much you need his help to draw your next breath and take your next step.
2. Make a list of three ways you can mirror God by being creative. Then go do those things well, not for the world's accolades but to worshipfully imitate your Creator.
3. Ask God to reveal the areas of your life where you are most prone to play God. Confess them to Christ.
4. All sin is a version of falling for the same old lie to be like God. Think of the top three sins you struggle with. Analyze how each of those sins is, on a deep level, an attempt to play God. Then, take a minute, and confess those sins to your Creator, trusting that his grace, offered in Christ, is more than enough to cover your sinful self-worship.
5. I offered the examples of Jim Morrison, Michel Foucault, and RuPaul as people pretending to be cutting edge but who in reality abide by the conventions of Genesis 3. Think of three living celebrities who embody the same sense of devil-may-care freedom and self-liberation. Pray for each of them by name.

Chapter 3

#followyourheart

Thou shalt obey your emotions at all costs.

*Follow your Heart, for your heart will always know
the answer. But if it tells you to strangle kittens or
something then don't follow it anymore. I mean
it's just a heart, right? It's not the Dalai Lama.*
—EDWARD MONKTON, ALTER EGO OF GILES ANDREAE

*They said boy you must follow your heart
But my heart just led me into my chest . . .
But the Father of hearts . . .
He's the one I have chosen
And I will follow him.*
—RICH MULLINS, SONGWRITER

Apple cofounder, black turtleneck enthusiast, and former Pixar chairman Steve Jobs once remarked, "There is no reason not to follow your heart."[1] The tech wizard clearly did not put as much thought into this statement as he did into his smartphones. The truth is, there are plenty of good reasons not to follow your heart.

For most of human history, feelings could be embraced, resisted, ignored, celebrated, chastened, silenced, trained, or challenged. Our ancestors could do a whole lot with their emotions. The "freedom" of our day is far more limiting. You have one option when it comes to your heart—follow it. If you are a male with a feeling that Brad Pitt or Tom Brady are physically attractive or a female who finds sex appeal in Margot Robbie or Rachel McAdams, then it cannot possibly be just a feeling that virtually anyone could acknowledge and move on with their lives. No. Those feelings must be taken as seriously as Christians take the Bible, Muslims take the Qur'an, or Jehovah's Witnesses take the Watchtower. Those feelings must be authoritative. Rather than simply being able to recognize attractiveness in both men and women, you must redefine your very identity in obedience to your feelings and come out as gay, bi, or pan. Anything less than full obedience and expression of each subjective feeling of sexual attraction would be an unforgivable sin against your very self. Take your every feeling, whim, or attraction so seriously that they have the unquestionable godlike power to define you. Anyone who tells you otherwise is a bigot, a phobic, a hater, or worse yet, a Republican.

It was unthinkable to historic humanity to grant our emotions our unwavering obedience. They understood what ten seconds of honest introspection reveals—our hearts can be *wrong*. Our ancestors tried to conform their disordered emotions to the world around them, not conform the world around them to their emotions. Aristotle encouraged his students to pursue "ordinate affections." Augustine called people to sync up their inner lives with the *ordo amoris*—that is, matching their affections with the actual loveworthiness of things. The Buddha called his devotees to question and transcend their emotional attachments. Islam called followers to a "greater jihad"—that is, the struggle against transgressive desires inside us. Early Hindus called this process *satya*. Chinese tradition called it the *Tao*. Christians call it discipleship or sanctification.

Our ancestors, like us, got many things wrong. But one thing they got right was that feelings were not the final word on reality. They could be valid or not. The difference was whether those feelings corresponded to metaphysical, moral, or aesthetic reality. In our day, we have turned that grand human tradition inside out. Life is no longer about bringing our inner selves into the tempo and key of beauty, goodness, and truth. It is now about finding our own inner tune, marching to our own beat, playing it loud, and conducting as much of the world around us as we can to play along with our anthems of autonomy.

Pulitzer Prize–winning author Anna Quindlen declared to a packed auditorium of graduates, "Look inside. That way lies dancing to the melodies spun out by your own heart."[2] This all sounds liberating and inspirational, but it is terrible advice. It is the cliché fluff of commencement addresses, Oscar acceptance speeches, yearbook inscriptions, and pop choruses. We don't hear such fuzzy sentiments from people who followed their hearts straight to the divorce court, the detox clinic, or the prison yard.

Dull

Our first reason to not follow our hearts, answering Steve Jobs, is that our hearts are too dull. Validating our every feeling seems exhilarating, at least at first. Yet we end up trapped inside our own mental constructs.[3] We become what David Foster Wallace called "lords of our tiny skull-sized kingdoms, alone at the center of all creation."[4] Looking inside our hearts does not give us limitless freedom so much as a bad case of claustrophobia.

Don't get me wrong, I have no doubt that your heart is fascinating. But compared with the heart of God—the God Augustine described well as "an infinite and unbounded ocean of being"[5]— our hearts hold all the thrill of a mossy fishbowl. That we would follow our own hearts over that of an infinitely interesting, creative, good, wise, just, loving, powerful, and joyful Being is strong evidence of just how absurdly shortsighted we are.

Dithering

Your heart, like mine, is not only too dull, it is also too dithering to follow. Our hearts flutter, waver, and vacillate. They are shifting sands—hardly solid bedrock on which to build our identities. Take stock of the emotions you've felt today. Ask yourself, "Do any of the bold words in the following list capture my self-directed emotions today?"

I felt pretty much **nothing**, like an emotionally dead fish.
I felt deeply **secure** in who I am and my life mission.
I felt **panicky** and **unsure** of myself.
I felt **angry** at myself.
I felt **confused** and **jumbled up inside**, getting mixed
   messages.

I felt **confident** and **optimistic**, like I could take on the world.

I felt **overwhelmed** and **drained**, like I'm sputtering on emotional fumes.

I felt **fun** and **attractive**, like someone others love having around.

I felt **isolated** and **lonesome**, like I haven't meaningfully connected with anyone in too long.

I felt **loved** and **valued**, like people around me want what's best for me.

I felt **anxiety** and **dread**, worrying about myself most of the day.

I felt **tranquil** and **rested**.

If you took the same emotional inventory a week, a month, or a year from now, what is the likelihood your answers would be identical? The truth is that our emotions can blip all over the radar. Heraclitus, the Greek philosopher, famously said you never step in the same river twice because it is always flowing. Our hearts are in constant flux. Some hearts may be as turbulent as the Ganges in monsoon season, and others move like molasses on a cold day, but all human hearts are in motion.

Now that we have some idea of what our own hearts say is true of us, let's compare that with what God says is true. We will focus on a single sentence from the opening chapter of Paul's letter to Ephesus, the longest sentence in the Bible, 204 words in the original Greek before Paul pauses to breathe. According to this glorious run-on sentence, if you trust in Christ instead of yourself, then you are . . .

. . . **blessed** with every spiritual blessing.

. . . **chosen** in Christ since before the world began.

. . . **holy** and **blameless** before him.

... **predestined** to be an **adopted** and **cherished** son or daughter of God.

... **blessed** with God's glorious grace in Christ.

... **redeemed** through Jesus's blood.

... **forgiven** of all your trespasses.

... **lavished** with the riches of God's grace.

... an **heir** with Christ, a recipient of the extravagant eternal rewards he earned.

... **predestined** into that inheritance by the same omnipotent God who works everything according to his will.

... **designed to praise his glory**.

... **sealed with the promised Holy Spirit,** who is strong and competent enough to guarantee our eternal inheritance.

Did you feel all twelve of those awesome truths today? If so, that's incredible. Be grateful. But likely you were not emotionally locked into those truths all day. We experience a slew of emotions that contradict who we are according to Ephesians 1. Which are you going to trust to tell you the truth about yourself—your own vacillating emotions or what God says? The truth is that what God says is true about you is infinitely more trustworthy than whatever your fallen feelings say from one moment to the next. If you don't want to end up in an eternal identity crisis, then don't follow *your* heart, follow his. Don't take your flowing feelings at their word, take God at his. His joyous verdict about you is trustworthy and solid as stone.

Divided

Not only are our hearts infinitely less steady and trustworthy than God, our hearts are also loaded with mixed messages. The follow-your-heart dogma naively assumes that our hearts are like a choir, with each of our emotions harmonizing with all other emotions. The truth is, our hearts are less like a choir and more like a Guitar Center storefront in which fifty guitarists on fifty different guitars and amps are all trying to out-shred one another.

In *The Abolition of Man*, C. S. Lewis captures the point using the language of "instinct." "Telling us to obey Instinct is like telling us to obey 'people.' People say different things: so do instincts. . . . Each instinct, if you listen to it, will claim to be gratified at the expense of all the rest."[6] Even Buddy Pine, the supervillain Syndrome from the Steve Jobs–greenlit film *The Incredibles*, gets the point. "You always say, 'Be true to yourself,'" Pine complains to his former idol Mr. Incredible, "but you never say which part of yourself to be true to!"[7] In choosing a life of cruelty, force, and deception, Buddy was indeed being true to parts of himself.[8]

Depraved

The call to cardiac obedience assumes that the human heart is not depraved. But the relapsing addict follows his heart. He *feels* entitled to another fix regardless of the devastation it will bring to his loved ones and his liver. The white supremacist follows his heart. He *feels* superior to people with more melanin in their skin cells, regardless of how absurd it is to make pigmentation a litmus test of human worth. Imperialist warlords, terrorists, con artists, thieves, pathological liars—

Under what mass hypnosis did we come to think of the human heart as some unquestionable beacon of moral virtue?

they all follow their hearts. Under what mass hypnosis did we come to think of the human heart as some unquestionable beacon of moral virtue?

We like to think we have advanced beyond the quaint superstitions of our ancestors, but they offer us a much needed dose of realism. "The heart is deceitful above all things, and desperately sick; who can understand it?" (Jer. 17:9) said the Jewish prophet. "The hearts of the children of man are full of evil, and madness is in their hearts while they live," (Eccl. 9:3) said the Jewish philosopher. "Out of the heart come evil thoughts, murder, adultery, sexual immorality, theft, false witness, slander," (Matt. 15:19–20) said the Jewish Messiah. Proverbs 28:26 sums it up bluntly: "One who trusts in his own heart is a fool" (NASB).

This indictment of the human heart will sound offensive and outdated if we have bought into the far more flattering doctrine of Jean-Jacques Rousseau. For Rousseau and his legions of disciples today, "there is no original perversity in the human heart. . . . Man is naturally good."[9] We like it when megachurch pastor Joel Osteen says we "don't do wrong on purpose" and our "heart is right."[10] Something inside us says "Amen" when the great philosopher Celine Dion tells us, "I don't think you can go wrong if you follow your heart."[11] Who, then, better understands human hearts—ancient Jews like Jeremiah, Solomon, and Jesus, or modern culture-shapers like Rousseau, Osteen, and Dion?

To answer that question, let us travel back to a time when the goodness of the human heart was widely celebrated—the French Enlightenment. We stroll along the banks of the Seine River, swept up in a procession of jubilant Parisians marching toward Notre Dame Cathedral. At the crest of the parade, we see a fourteen-year-old actress hoisted on the shoulders of some French men. Her name is Mademoiselle Candeille. She is dressed as the Goddess of Reason. We follow the crowd into the cathedral and shuffle across the black-and-white checkered tiles to behold the teenager posing atop the high altar. The Parisians break out in song, singing humanistic hymns for their new goddess. It is the year 1792. The air is full of adrenaline and a wild hope of what glories lie ahead as humanity shakes off the shackles of the old religion, with its depressing doctrines about human depravity. One French revolutionary, Marquis de Condorcet, sums up the new optimism well: "The moral goodness of man . . . is capable of indefinite perfection like all his other faculties."[12]

Now let's click our time destination dials just a few months forward to 1793. We walk those same Paris streets, only this time we're ankle-deep in blood. What had been hailed as the age of reason devolved within a few months to the age of the guillotine. Blades fell all over France. Condorcet, for all his optimistic praise of humanity's unlimited moral perfectibility, was found hanging lifeless in a prison cell while awaiting his own turn at the guillotine. His capital crime wasn't crossing the church; it was committing heresies against his fellow secular humanists, flexing their newfound power.

I am not arguing that we can lay all atrocities at the feet of those evil secularists. Religious folks have unleashed plenty of horrors on humanity.[13] It doesn't take a PhD in theology to see that burning "witches," sending kids to fight crusades, wearing bed sheets to lynch Black people, and a thousand other "church"-sponsored injustices are fundamentally incompatible with Jesus's life and teachings. The common denominator between religious and secular carnage is neither religion nor secularity, it is *people*. We use a range of contradictory ideologies as an excuse to express the moral insanity in our hearts.

Delusional

Some may bristle, thinking, "There are maniacs and bullies in the world. But they are flukes. Rousseau was right. Most people are basically good." This objection almost always comes with the important caveat, "*I* am part of that basically good crowd, not the maniac, bully crowd." What we're up against here is one of the most documented findings in social science, a phenomenon known as "the self-serving bias." Psychologist David Meyers captures the self-serving bias by noting, "When I win at Scrabble it's because of my verbal dexterity; when I lose it is because, 'Who could get anywhere with a Q but no U?'"[14]

Most Americans view themselves as more intelligent, more ethical, and less prejudiced than their neighbors and peers.[15] Ninety-four percent of college professors believe themselves to be superior to their average colleagues.[16] One College Board survey asked 829,000 high school seniors to rate their ability to get along with others. One hundred percent ranked themselves "above average," while 25 percent ranked themselves in the top 1 percent.[17]

Here we have another case of the science catching up with the Scriptures. "Every way of a man is right in his own eyes" (Prov. 21:2). This self-serving bias is one of the main reasons that the call to follow our hearts does not strike us as silly as it actually is. If your heart is basically good, then, as Steve Jobs said, there is no good reason to not follow it.

The evidence, however, is stacked against us. In a Yale University basement in 1961, Stanley Milgram conducted one of the most famous psychological experiments of all time. His subjects were not sociopaths or death row inmates. They were average Joes and Janes. He found that a majority of everyday folks would be willing to jolt the bodies of strangers with potentially lethal voltage. All it took was minimal pressure from an authority figure. (Thankfully the shock victims were actors and not actually fried alive by strangers.)

Ten years later came the controversial Stanford Prison Experiment. Philip Zimbardo selected two dozen psychologically fit young men with no criminal records for a two-week study of behavior in a simulated prison environment. After dividing the subjects as either guards or prisoners, things went *Lord of the Flies* quickly. Within twenty-four hours of the "prisoners'" mock arrests, the "guards" sprayed them with fire extinguishers, stripped them nude, took their mattresses away, and threw unruly prisoners into solitary confinement. The next day the guards withheld prisoners' bathroom privileges in favor of buckets. Coming days brought so much brutality that authorities had to step in and end the experiment. Again, these were not deviants or criminals; they were average folks like you and me.

If you still doubt we are capable of far more inhumanity than we care to admit, I encourage you to attend a Black Friday blowout sale the midnight after Thanksgiving. The human heart can flip from gratitude to greed in a matter of milliseconds. Still not convinced? Watch an episode of *Dance Moms*. Attend a church-sponsored Easter egg hunt. Introspect for ten honest seconds. Scripture clarifies: "None is righteous, no, not one" (Rom. 3:10). We are far more corrupt and corruptible than we like to admit.

We are far more corrupt and corruptible than we like to admit.

Who had it right when it comes to the human heart? The answer comes from an unlikely source. Hard-core atheist Michael Ruse concluded,

> I think Christianity is spot on about original sin. How could one think otherwise, when the world's most civilized and advanced people (the people of Beethoven, Goethe, Kant) embraced that slime-ball Hitler and participated in the Holocaust? I think Saint Paul and the great Christian philosophers had real insights into sin and freedom and responsibility, and I want to build on this rather than turn from it.[18]

The Wisdom of a Nine-Year-Old

Recall my nine-year-old's insight from the dedication of this book: "I don't want to follow my own heart. My heart is fallen. I'd way rather follow God's heart!" We can now better appreciate Dutch's insightfulness. Our hearts are dull. Better to follow the least boring Being in existence. Our hearts are dithering. Better to follow the heart of Someone who is unmovable in his loving commitment toward us. Our hearts are divided. Better to follow the heart of Someone who is utterly unified in his passion for his glory and mission for our good. Our hearts are depraved. Better to follow the heart of Someone with real moral credibility, a God who is altogether good and holy. Our hearts are delusional. Better to follow the heart of Someone who sees us at our absolute, unfiltered worst and still loves us beyond measure. Trust the Lord's bedrock promises, not your sandy perceptions. If you want to truly find yourself, don't take your own heart nearly as seriously as you take your Creator's.

A Heretic's Testimonial

Jamal Bandy is a Bible teacher and podcaster at *Prescribed Truth* who hails from Columbus, Georgia. He is also a heretic against the cult of self-worship. He boldly breaks the #followyourheart commandment. This is his story.

For far too long I lived my life by the advice of strangers to follow my heart. I can testify from personal experience: it is truly terrible advice. It left me lost and confused. It had me bouncing in all directions with no true foundation to stand on. When I was growing up, my dad parented me with a kind of follow-your-heart parenting philosophy, supporting whatever career path my heart nudged me toward, no questions asked. First, it was to become a professional musician. When that buzz wore off, I wanted to be an architect. My dad would buy the necessary equipment and pay for whatever classes I needed. Then, after a few months, I wouldn't "feel it" anymore and would move on. What a colossal waste of time, energy, and money!

Following my heart was no better for my relationships than it was for my career aspirations. As I pursued romantic connections with the opposite sex, my feelings toward them were anything but solid. My heart would shift from one moment to the next, and my trying to follow the moving target of my emotions left the women around me hurt and confused. Why do we almost never consider the pain and trauma that following our hearts can cause others? Given the unpredictability of my heart, and mistaking certain fleeting feelings with true love, I was left wondering whether I could ever love anyone at all.

Things weren't going any better when I pursued meaningful relationships in the friendship department. There were plenty of times when I knew my friends were in need and I would desire to help them. But the next minute, that desire would fade, my heart would change, and I would avoid their calls. Following my heart meant I couldn't be depended on and set many of my relationships on a course for disaster.

As if the thrashing of my career path and relationships wasn't enough, my sense of self was also left in shambles. How I viewed myself would change by the hour. One moment I felt unsure of myself. The next moment my heart would burst with confidence, which would shortly vanish without a trace. How could I truly know myself if my heart sent so many contradictory messages about myself?

Is there any good news here or just a long, sad trail of damage? The good news is that, through no power or goodness of my own, I experienced the saving grace of Jesus Christ. It rocked me. It transformed and deepened my understanding of love. Being loved by a God who is consistent, perfect, and faithful helped me realize how weak, unorganized, and untrustworthy my heart has been all along. Now my identity is secure in Christ, who is my deepest source of joy and satisfaction. My relationships have blossomed as I seek not to obey my fickle, self-centered heart but to obey God's call to serve others and love my neighbors. I'm no longer drowning in uncertainty about my future. Knowing that an omniscient God ordered my steps from the foundation of the world gives me steady assurance when things don't go as I planned. Unlike your heart, God can lead you perfectly and without fail.

—Jamal

A Heretic's Prayer

God,
Your heart is infinitely exhilarating, unwavering, unified, and
good. Given who you are, it cannot be otherwise. Our hearts
can be dull, dithering, divided, depraved, and delusional. That
we would follow our hearts instead of yours is absurd. But we
do it anyway. We fall back on our fallen perceptions rather

than your promises, and that silly, misplaced trust renders us far more anxious and depressed than we need to be. Help us to resist the spirit of the age by not taking our feelings as the final word on reality. That doesn't mean we cut off our emotions. You made us to be more than brains floating in vats. Instead, we ask you to be Lord over our hearts. Reshape our affections so that instead of us glorifying our feelings we would use our feelings to glorify you. Amen.

A Heretic's Field Manual

Before moving on to the next chapter, do at least three of the following to sharpen your skills at violating the commandment to #followyourheart:

1. Identify at least three feelings you had today that were false, misguided, or likely to change tomorrow. Think of one example of a feeling you had today that was *way* off. Have a chuckle at yourself.
2. Think of a recurring lie your heart tells you about yourself that may often feel true but you know is false. Search the Scriptures, using a search engine or concordance if helpful, and find at least three Spirit-inspired passages that contradict that lie.
3. Take five minutes to write out a meaningful message to someone you know who could use some encouragement, especially if you don't want to. Send it.
4. Have a conversation with someone in which you ask them meaningful questions about their life and listen. Do not turn the conversation back to yourself at any point.

5. Ask the Holy Spirit to fill your heart with his fruits. Prayerfully request love, joy, peace, patience, kindness, gentleness, goodness, faithfulness, and self-control.

Chapter 4

#betruetoyourself

Thou shalt be courageous enough to
defy others' expectations.

If you follow your heart, you don't need to follow anyone.
—DEEPTI RAGHAV, BOLLYWOOD PRODUCER

I know of men who believe in themselves more
colossally than Napoleon or Caesar. I know
where flames the fixed star of certainty and
success. I can guide you to the thrones of the
Super-men. The men who really believe in
themselves are all in lunatic asylums.
—G. K. CHESTERTON, BRITISH HUMORIST

I was a mostly clueless seventeen-year-old when I had one of my first genuine philosophical insights. Dr. Chris, my humanities teacher, had finished a unit on the thought of Friedrich Nietzsche. Nietzsche despised cows—that is, anyone who mindlessly follows the herd rather than charting their own course. The *Übermenschen*, the heroic supermen of Nietzsche's universe, brazenly defy the moral expectations of others. They possess the courage and will-power to do their own thing.

If I committed myself to Nietzsche's call to radical self-expression, wouldn't I be abiding by this dead German's dogmas, following someone else's demands on my existence like a good little cow? I posed the question to Dr. Chris after class. "Wouldn't following Nietzsche's philosophy make me less of a superman to the extent that I seek to live out *his* vision for *my* life?" I was met with a look from Dr. Chris that said, "Welcome to philosophy. Congrats on finding your first of many contradictions." I had no idea at the time that this catch-22 in Nietzsche's thought would go so far to explain the most pressing contradictions of our culture some twenty-five years later.

Gonna Have to Serve Someone

It was that same humanities class in 1997 where I attempted to explain the good news of Jesus to a friend named "Mike." Mike replied with a line borrowed from the lips of Milton's Lucifer in *Paradise Lost*: "I'd rather reign in hell than serve in heaven!" Mike, who had apparently taken to our lesson on Nietzsche with great enthusiasm, would serve no one but Mike.

It wasn't until years later when I heard Bob Dylan's Grammy-winning single "Gotta Serve Somebody" that the problem with Mike's Luciferian-Nietzschean credo of self-rule became obvious. Dylan sings about big shot politicians, heavyweight champions, rock stars, warlords, business moguls, network executives, mansion-dwelling fat cats, and more. Many of those Dylan puts on exhibition for us are poster boys for the modern idea of freedom. They have the power and fortune to fulfill their every personal desire. But Dylan, as only Dylan can do, subverts the status quo and makes doubters of us all. He rips the shiny veneer off Western values to expose their contradictions: "Well, it may be the devil or it may be the Lord, but you're gonna have to serve somebody."[1] For Dylan, the sultans may be the real slaves. We can think we are our own masters when we're really unwitting servants of a dark kingdom.[2]

> You're gonna have to serve somebody.

Think of Dylan's insight this way: The whole world is like a super-store. There are twenty-seven varieties of toothpaste to choose from, seventy-four iterations of condensed soup, nine styles of orange juice (each available in eight size options). We are inundated with options to express our personal pleasure preferences. The same holds true for how we seek, or rather how we *shop*, for meaning. "Shopping" is not only the right word for how we acquire toothpaste and orange juice, it also describes a total life orientation.[3]

Products often have hidden ingredients—aspartame, nitrates, and MSG to name a few. It's the same with worldviews. They have ingredients that few people realize are baked into their chosen systems of meaning. To Dylan's point, every conceivable code of living you could choose has one ingredient that you rarely see advertised on the front of the box—that is, *service*. There simply is no worldview on the market with the ingredient (in reality) of absolute freedom by which you can invent your own identity and be obedient to none but yourself. Such an ingredient is as illusory as cheeseburgers and fries that give you chiseled abs.

Meet Your Masters

Most of those seeking to stay true to themselves likely don't know the names of those who framed their worldview, but they follow their dogmas all the same. If I believe that my heart is basically good, a reliable guide to the good life, then I am unwittingly paying service to people whom most have never heard of, including Pelagius, Rousseau, and Joel Osteen.

If I spurn all religious authority to chart my own path, I am hardly the rebel I think I am. I am paying homage with a pinch of incense to Lord Byron, Arthur Rimbaud, Voltaire, and others.

If I believe I have a duty to shatter taboos and authentically express my sexual appetites, then I am hardly the brave space monkey I think I am. I am a sheep herded by shepherds like Marquis de Sade, Wilhelm Reich, Alfred Kinsey, Michel Foucault, and Freddie Mercury.

If I believe I can define my gender, then I am hardly the self-defining revolutionary I think I am. I am reciting the doctrines of John Money and other gender ideologues like a faithful fundamentalist.

Those who believe they can chart the meanings of their own lives are hardly captains of their own souls. They are crewmates scrubbing the poop decks on the SS *Nietzsche*, SS *Sartre*, or the far more colorful, rainbow-sailed SS *RuPaul*.

We are up against what we could call the "punk rocker's paradox." Punk rock was originally formed as a spit wad in the eyeball of the establishment, a rebel yell for nonconformity. Attend a punk rock show. You will behold a crowd that is so nonconformist that their black outfits, dyed hair, and metal accessories make them virtually interchangeable with one other. A square with the courage to brandish a pressed collared shirt, khakis, and a crew cut would be the only true punk rocker in a sea of posers, all dutifully wearing their corporate Hot Topic uniforms. "I'm so unique, just like everyone else!" Dylan was right. You are gonna have to serve somebody. It may be the devil and his proxies or it may be the Lord, but you are gonna have to serve.

Murphy's Dilemma

Picture a Northern Irish teen called Murphy. Coming of age in 1970s Belfast, especially after Bloody Sunday, which claimed 13 civil rights protestors, we could understand why a desire to unleash aggression against the Brits would beat strong in Murphy's heart. Should Murphy look within for answers and follow his heart?

Now let's transplant Murphy to an American university today. Here he is warned over and over by those in authority about the dangers of what has been branded "toxic masculinity." He once found a military career to be a noble and adventurous life path but has found a new, competing desire in his heart to unleash his inner interpretive dancer, a desire his gender studies professor strongly encouraged. Should Murphy be true to himself?

In both scenarios, whether the streets of Belfast or the halls of the gender studies department, telling Murphy to be true to himself is hardly the call to unfettered self-definition that it's cracked up to be. If he takes the advice, he will end up a walking paradox, thinking he's strolling freely when he's really marching to the beat of someone else's drum.

If a teenager desires to experiment sexually but also desires to uphold sex as something sacred and reserved for marriage, it is obvious which set of desires those telling her to follow her heart would consider to be from her real heart. She will believe she is being true to herself and free from social constraints, when she is really a pawn in a sexual agenda invented by Alfred Kinsey, Wilhelm Reich, Herbert Marcuse, Judith Butler, John Money, and other ideologues she's never heard of.[4]

We never seek to be true to ourselves in a vacuum. Our so-called true selves are shaped by cultural forces around us and what the elite say should be celebrated and what should be censored. Being true to ourselves is almost always a matter of being true to others.

Why would you obey the demands to be true to yourself when those demands usually come from marketing teams trying to maximize clicks and sell units, ideologues looking for sheep, influencers looking for likes, and entertainers desperate for relevance? What makes you think the trendsetters behind autocardiac obedience are your friends? What credible case can you build that the people who want you to be true to yourself even remotely have your good in mind?

The Proof of the Pudding Is in the Eating

Jesus warned us, "Beware of false prophets, who come to you in sheep's clothing but inwardly are ravenous wolves. You will recognize them by their fruits" (Matt. 7:15–16). What fruit did the prophets of self-worship produce in their own lives? If being true to ourselves is all it's cracked up to be, we should expect the architects of this ideology to have enjoyed the sweet fruit of joyously liberated lives, the kind of lives we would want for ourselves. History tells a different story.

Nero (AD 37–68) turned his self-worship into the official faith of the Roman Empire. He murdered his mother, Agrippina the

Younger, his first wife, Octavia, and, by some accounts, his second wife, Poppaea Sabina. He drained Roman resources building a golden house in his own honor, killed his critics, and, as his popularity waned, killed himself at the age of thirty.

Jean-Jacques Rousseau (1712–78) helped inspire the French Revolution and lay the philosophical foundation for the sexual revolution and left-wing politics.[5] "All I need to do," wrote Rousseau, "is to look inside myself."[6] His goal was to "make known my inner self, exactly as it was in every circumstance of my life," making him a forefather to the incessant autobiography and stream-of-consciousness emotional broadcasting found throughout the blogosphere and social media. Rousseau believed people are basically good and blamed social structures for all evil. With an eye toward his own freedom and self-expression, he abandoned all five of his children to early deaths at an orphanage.

Friedrich Nietzsche (1844–1900) called people beyond what he saw as the slave morality of a meek Christianity to embrace a strong-willed master morality (*herrenmoral*). He mocks the "herds" and celebrates "him who breaketh up their tables of values, the breaker, the lawbreaker,"[7] the man who "plays the game of creating new values."[8] After a deeply lonesome life, Nietzsche spent his last decade in an asylum, known for dancing naked, fantasizing about shooting the kaiser, and believing himself to be Jesus Christ, Napoleon, Buddha, and other historical figures.[9]

Michel Foucault (1926–1984), a devotee of Nietzsche, saw sexual experiences as the path to self-glorification, calling us "to exchange life in its entirety for sex itself, for the truth and the sovereignty of sex."[10] He battled suicidal tendencies most of his adult life. He argued for "consensual" sexual relations between adults and children, campaigning for the legalization of pedophilia in France.[11] When he relocated to Berkeley, California, Foucault threw himself into the sadomasochistic homosexual scene. Sadly, he contracted

HIV/AIDS and, like Queen's Freddie Mercury, continued to gratify his sexual appetites even after he knew he was infected. When Foucault said, "Sex is worth dying for,"[12] he practiced what he preached, not only for himself but for unsuspecting others.

Aleister Crowley (1875–1947) added an occultic element to self-worship, inventing a religion called "Thelema" (from the Greek noun for "will, want, and desire"). Crowley distilled the dogmas of his faith to the command, "Do what thou wilt." He expounded, "Only you can ascertain your own True Will; no god, no man, no institution or nation surpasses your Holy Authority over yourself." His biographer described him as "brash, eccentric, egotistic, highly intelligent, arrogant, witty, wealthy, and, when it suited him, cruel."[13] He was "capable of immense physical and emotional cruelty."[14] In doing what he willed, Crowley became a heroin addict, physically assaulted his lovers (male and female), and appreciated both Nazism and Communism for their deeply anti-Christian themes.[15]

Jean-Paul Sartre (1905–1980) was one of the luminaries of French existentialism, "the first principle" of which is that "man is nothing else but what he makes himself."[16] We exist in a godless universe, and it is therefore up to us to invent our own essences. What did Sartre make of himself? He was known for a vast ego and as a notorious womanizer, with a revolving door of mistresses he famously treated more like prey than people. It wasn't about "physical pleasure," for Sartre, "it was about the thrill of the chase, the almost sadistic conquest of another."[17] He was known to pop up to 50 pills a day, got hooked on amphetamines, hid vodka behind his books to help him get blackout drunk, and talked often with imaginary visitors.[18] Hardly the poster boy of boundless freedom he had advertised to a generation of adoring youth, he confessed, "I'm gaga, as they say. Or, I'm not stupid. But I'm empty. . . . There are not many things left that excite me."[19]

Timothy Leary (1920–1996) was a Harvard professor and apostle of the hippie generation who famously told thirty thousand youth in San Francisco's Golden Gate Park to "turn on, tune in, and drop out."[20] He championed psychedelic drugs as the pathway to ultimate self-realization. He advocated for contaminating America's water supply with LSD to usher in the utopian Age of Aquarius. Eventually Leary's drug consumption robbed him of his brilliant mind, as it became clear in his later interviews that the lights were on but, tragically, no one was home. A former student of mine named Toby owned a home in Laguna Beach, California. Leary and other figureheads of the psychedelic movement would frequently crash at his home. Toby recounted to me, with tears in his eyes, how terrible it was to watch Leary and many of his devotees collapse under the weight of the ideology of psychedelic self-realization.

If you believe I have merely cherry-picked the least flattering cases, then I encourage you to read up on the personal lives of other saints of self-worship—Marquis de Sade, Alfred Kinsey, Jim Morrison, L. Ron Hubbard, Wilhelm Reich, Jacques Derrida, or whoever else you can find who helped shape today's zeitgeist of radical expressive individualism. We know a tree by its fruits and the fruits of these men's lives should be enough to give us pause before we embrace their calls to be true to ourselves.

The point of these sad stories is not to high-five one another and scoff at the woes of those whose self-worship contributed to their own demise. Each of these broken men was an image-bearer of God. We should weep, not snicker, at great minds that crashed and burned because they navigated life by an inverted horizon with themselves at the top and God at the bottom.

The point of these grim biographies is also not to pretend that every influential Christian has lived an exemplary life. Many have not. Rather, the point is Jesus himself. Jesus calls us not to be true to ourselves but to be true to his Father, like he was. He never murdered his competitors, treated people like sex toys, indulged sadistic or suicidal urges, fried his brain cells with drugs, pushed a murderous political ideology, or became a paranoid, easily offended egomaniac. Human history has never known anyone so utterly good. Since, as

The point is Jesus himself.

we have seen, we've gotta serve someone, I'd rather be true to Christ than the motley and miserable crew who want me to be true to them.

You Gotta Have Faith, Faith, Faith

In the late 1980s George Michael sang, "I gotta have faith, faith, faith." There's something deeper to that lyric than perhaps the former Wham! singer intended. The old Greek word for "faith"—*pistis*—simply means "trust." After a decade of teaching atheists, I am clear on this: There is no such thing as someone *losing* their faith. Rather, people *relocate* their faith to another object.

Many who find the invitation to trust Jesus to be a threat to their self-determination aren't faithless. Whether in a political ideology, a romance, the voice within, or the dogmas of the influencers explored previously, they place their trust elsewhere.[21] These new objects of faith are almost never scrutinized like the previous object of faith. If they were, many would find they had stepped not from a rocking boat onto solid ground but into a churning sea. Thankfully, some who walk away from faith because of the evils done to them in Jesus's name eventually do scrutinize their subsequent faiths and circle back to encounter the love, healing, and grace of the real Jesus. I was raised by two such people.

Many of my friends had their faith severely undermined by representatives of that faith. One friend who bailed on Christianity was sexually abused by a trusted youth leader during an overnighter. Another found that a trusted Christian media personality had been siphoning millions of dollars from the ministry she worked for. Others walked away when their church leaders met honest questions with threats of eternal damnation or exorcisms to expel the demons of doubt. It is no small matter when people who claim to represent Christ break trust and perpetrate injustice in his name. For many, that broken trust is devastating. I have experienced several ministries where if those in charge were accurate representatives of Jesus, I would want nothing to do with Jesus.

Would it be reasonable to never watch another movie because Harvey Weinstein was a sexual predator, never enjoy a Beatles album because Phil Spector was a murderer, or never eat another hoagie because Subway's former spokesman Jared was a pedophile? We are adept at separating babies from bathwater, except, for some reason, when it comes to faith.

Those representing—or rather, misrepresenting—Christ are not Christ. The actual Jesus willfully entered flesh in a pain-ridden world. He successfully endured temptation, the sting of public humiliation, and the ire of the religious elite. He felt anxiety to the point of sweating blood. His nerve endings jolted as thorns pierced his temples, a splintered crossbar was laid on his lashed back, railroad spikes severed his wrists and ankles, and a spear entered his rib cage. He then asphyxiated on a Roman cross. *That* Jesus is not the person who hurt you. *That* Jesus is the one who loves you beyond your comprehension. *That* Jesus would never con, abuse, swindle, deceive, or dehumanize you.

Putting your faith in him is worlds apart from putting your faith in anyone who damaged you in Jesus's name. Moving your faith away from him on account of people who violated you by violating his teachings is not your best path forward. Every worldview has its share of wolves, con artists, perverts, and hypocrites. Christianity is most fundamentally a call not to intellectually assent to a man-made worldview, but to yield relationally to a real, resurrected person. You can scour the earth, sit at the feet of gurus, tune in for the most enlightening podcasts—you will find no one as challenging enthralling, unpredictable, substantial, and virtuous as Jesus. He can enlighten and expand your mind and soul like no other. Seeking to be true to him is far more life-giving than being true to others' selves under the guise of being true to yourself.

You will find no one as challenging, enthralling, unpredictable, substantial and virtuous Jesus.

Capes or Cowbells?

Which would you rather be—a cow or Superman? The bovine life comes with time to roam, chew cud, stare at hills, and let the wind cool your leather. There would be far fewer demands on your time from damsels on train tracks or school children in sinking buses. But then again, your cow self wouldn't be faster than a speeding bullet, more powerful than a locomotive, or able to leap tall buildings in a single bound. You would barely even realize you're a cow.

Nietzsche, we might argue, rules much of TikTok and indeed much of today's Western world from the grave. The prolific German atheist took the iconoclast's hammer to the concept of an objective moral structure in which human beings flourish. He deconstructed the classical Christian virtues, like humility and altruism, which he saw as a herd morality that left humanity compliant like cows. In his tome *Beyond Good and Evil*, Nietzsche declared, "The noble type of man feels *himself* to be the determiner of values.... Everything he knows to be part of himself, he honors: such a morality is self-glorification."[22]

In *Thus Spake Zarathustra*, Nietzsche spoke of "the three metamorphoses of the spirit." We start out as camels—that is, the "load-bearing spirit" burdened by traditional moral demands. Then we become lions who devour morality to "give a holy Nay to duty." The final and ideal stage for Nietzsche, the way to become a true *Übermensch*, is to become a "child" who plays "the game of creating new values."[23] There is a hair's breadth between Nietzsche's call to "let the value of everything be determined anew by you!" and the false "be true to yourself" gospel that pervades our culture.

As one wanders the post-Christian landscape of TikTok, where influencers flaunt their trans-species identities as cats and dogs, it is not hard to see a children's game of pretend extended into adulthood. As it has become trendy to hoist the Creator-sized task of creating an identity onto the shoulders of creatures, the question arises: "Are there enough self-glorifying value-creating supermen in the twenty-first century to form the new herd?" In Nietzsche's day it took a certain amount of countercultural willpower to spurn traditional moral expectations. Today, shunning traditional morality to create your own values is hardly risky or countercultural. You are given a warm welcome into the herd. The nineteenth-century superman must trade his cape for a cowbell if he continues to champion self-determined value in the twenty-first century. Resisting the herd's push toward self-glorification requires the very kind of subversive feat of will that Nietzsche applauded. The nineteenth-century cow becomes a twenty-first-century superman.

How, then, do we become a generation that soars above the herd and beckons others to trade their cowbells for capes? We worship a God who, unlike the self, is actually worthy of our worship. We become countercultural by aligning ourselves with transcendent beauty, goodness, truth, and justice. We refuse to moo along with the herd that makes their imperfect feelings the sacrosanct standard of truth. We expose how utterly hollow, bankrupt, and soul-crushing it is to follow Nero, Rousseau, Nietzsche, Foucault, Crowley, Sartre, and Leary in their philosophies of self-exaltation. We seek supernatural help to conform our fallen hearts to the heart of God. God, help us to be so awestruck with Christ that others are compelled to abandon their bovine existence to follow the most super of all supermen.

A Heretic's Testimonial

J. P. Moreland is ranked among *Time* magazine's one hundred top living philosophers. He serves as distinguished professor of philosophy at Biola University's Talbot School of Theology. He is also a heretic to the cult of self-worship. He boldly breaks the #betruetoyourself commandment. This is his story.

I became a Christian in November 1968. Since then, I have learned to avoid loneliness by drawing close to Jesus as my Lord and friend. I have found stability through troubled waters by practicing biblical gratitude. I found a wife, Hope, who had made the same commitment to Christ. Our marriage—forty-five years and counting—is founded upon Someone greater than we are, which has helped us weather our share of storms.

In August 2014, I began a three-year period in which I endured ten surgeries and three types of cancer. The possibility of immanent death was very real. But—and this is no kidding—all during that time, I experienced joy, happiness, and peace like never before. I experienced God's presence in the middle of otherwise terrifying circumstances. If I had lived for my own wants and desires, I would have fallen apart. I am convinced to my core—intellectually and experientially—that Christ offers us the most profound way to experience our human nature, by far.

As we seek to be our true selves through the travails of life, there is a pressing question we all must answer: *Do we, as human beings, have natures?* That may seem like a strange and abstract question, but your answer can make or break you. Let me explain. If something has a nature, that nature dictates the boundaries within which it thrives. Ignoring those boundaries brings harm. A dog, for example, has a nature by which it achieves canine flourishing. Stick it in a small cage all the time, feed it garbage, never pet it, or force it to live under water, and things won't go well.

Since we have natures, "freedom" means the power to do what we were made to do. If we pretend we don't have natures, then we reduce "freedom" to the right to do whatever we want. The results of this new nature-less "freedom" (which is just bondage renamed) have been nothing short of catastrophic. Forty million Americans report a major episode of clinical anxiety or depression each year. Suicide rates among teenagers—especially teenage girls—are at the highest rate ever recorded. Addictions are rampant, guys are increasingly preferring pornography to dating, and on and on. As the record-breaking numbers reveal, the #betruetoyourself notion of creating our own identities runs contrary to the loving boundaries God built into human nature for our joy and flourishing.

As a professional philosopher, I close with a warning: Don't be stupid. Don't waste your life trying to conjure up an identity from scratch. Remember, those who live by this commandment—shunning their Creator and defying their own created nature—die by this commandment. After fifty-four years of following Jesus, I can tell you without reservation that being true to Christ is far better than doing your own thing. Let's give ourselves anew to him today, as I did in 1968. Our often ignored and betrayed natures will thank us.

—J. P.

A Heretic's Prayer

Dear God,

We've gotta serve somebody. Thinking we can fabricate our own realities, our own identities, and our own meanings out of thin air is a delusion. When we try to be true to ourselves, we are almost always being true to the selves of others, pledging our obedience to those whose own lives were in shambles as they tried to be true to their own selves. We have no good reason to think that those who want us to be true to ourselves actually care in any meaningful sense about our well-being and thriving. But you, oh Lord, care. You care infinitely more about our good than we do. You have gone to astonishingly great lengths—in the incarnation, the crucifixion, and the resurrection—to bring us redemption and life. No philosopher, no self-help guru, no celebrity, no advertising strategist has even come close to what you have taken upon yourself for our good. Help us to be true to you, who love us even more than we love ourselves. Amen.

A Heretic's Field Manual

Before moving on to the next chapter, do at least three of the following to sharpen your skills at violating the commandment to #betruetoyourself:

1. Pick one of the four gospels—Matthew, Mark, Luke, or John. Find a Bible that sets Jesus's words apart in red. Carve out about an hour to do nothing but read through all the red letters in a given gospel. Then ask yourself, "What would it mean to be true to Jesus's heart for my life? How is his vision for my life better than my own?"
2. Ask God to clean your heart and to recalibrate your affections so that they align with those of Jesus.
3. Identify one bad action your heart is drawn to. Ponder what the opposite of that action might be, then go do it.
4. Give away something that means a lot to you; give it to someone it would mean even more to.
5. Do something kind that you don't really feel like doing for a member of your family.

#youdoyou

Thou shalt live your truth and let others live theirs.

*[A claim to be] "the Truth" sounds a little Mafioso
to me. You know, to each their own way.*
—MIKE DIRNT, GREEN DAY BASSIST

*The new rebel is a Skeptic. . . . And the fact that he
doubts everything really gets in his way when he wants
to denounce anything. For all denunciation implies a
moral doctrine of some kind. . . . Therefore the modern
man in revolt has become practically useless for all
purposes of revolt. By rebelling against everything
he has lost his right to rebel against anything.*
—G. K. CHESTERTON, CHEESE CONNOISSEUR

Everybody needs something, you know? If it's Jesus, if it's Satan, if it's alcohol, if it's music, whatever."[1] If indeed each individual stands as his, her, or zer own supreme meaning-maker, then Drowning Pool lead singer Dave Williams was right to say this. We find this "whatever" worldview captured in hashtags like #youdoyou and popular clichés like "live your truth," "that's true for you but not for me," "never judge others," and "different strokes for different folks." For those who buy into these polite, philosophically loaded slogans, the only sin is calling anything sin. Why shouldn't everyone live their own truth?

The Attempted Assassination of Venus

To understand how the doctrine of the sovereign self leads to this kind of trendy and seemingly tolerant whateverism, we begin on the five-hundred-year-old canvas of Titian. Titian the Italian master painted another artist in the creative process, a musician composing a song on his lute. Our young musician gazes over his right shoulder to behold a reclining woman, wearing jewelry and nearly nothing else. Was there some strange custom of musicians gazing at women *au naturel*? No, something else is going on here. Renaissance artists revived mythic gods and goddesses from Greco-Roman antiquity as visual symbols for whatever invisible realities they wanted to capture on canvas. Try drawing an abstract value like liberty. Good luck. It is easier to draw a towering woman in a spiked hat with a raised torch. Try sketching romantic love. A winged baby with a bow and arrow might help. Rather than painting the notion of objective

Public Domain/Metropolitan Museum of Art

Venus and the Lute Player

beauty, it is much simpler to paint a reclining nude deity named Venus as a stand-in for beauty. That is exactly what Titian did in his appropriately titled *Venus and the Lute Player.*

For Titian, the true artist is transfixed by a beauty beyond himself. He finds creative inspiration not in self-obsession but in the objectively beautiful. Dutch art critic Hans Rookmaaker remarked, "[Titian's] was a world in which it was possible to speak of the reality of such concepts as beauty or love. They were realities outside man. . . . Love and beauty were not just man's feelings and man's subjective taste; they were really there: if he did not follow them, hate and ugliness would be the result."[2]

With Rookmaaker's insight, the meaning of Titian's canvas opens up to us. Titian's musician is not some kind of twenty-first-century pop star merely using the power of sound to broadcast his or her intense feelings to consumers. Titian reminds us today that we must, like the lute player, look beyond ourselves. There is beauty, truth, love, and justice that we don't invent but discover. They were here long before we were born and would still be here if we all went belly-up tomorrow. We further damage the world when we don't sync our lives to the rhythm of those realities.

There is beauty, truth, love, and justice that we don't invent but discover.

It did not make headlines, but one of the most significant events of the twentieth century was the attempted murder of Venus.[3] In fact, the last century has witnessed multiple assassination attempts not only against Venus (beauty) but also against Veritas with her virginity and white robes (truth), Cupid with his bow and wings (love), and Themis with her blindfold and scales (justice). In the previous chapter we met some of their unhappy assassins. When it comes to beauty, they tell us, "there are no *a priori* aesthetic values."[4] Truth becomes "[nothing] more than what our peers . . . will let us get away with saying."[5] Love reduces to "two minutes and fifty-two seconds of squishing noises,"[6] and ethics "an illusion fobbed on us by our genes."[7] As for justice, "there is no standard, not even a divine one, against which the decisions of a free people can be measured."[8]

The extent to which we indulge in self-worship is the extent to which we become coconspirators to kill Venus, Veritas, Cupid, and Themis. The existence of transcendent beauty, truth, love, and justice is inconvenient. Their ongoing, living power calls us to look *above* ourselves. The true self-worshiper would never risk a crick in their neck or a lightly bruised kneecap. It's far easier to look *within* ourselves. Once a culture tries to bury Venus, Veritas, Cupid, and Themis, it is only a matter of time until it resurrects Narcissus or Kratos to take their place. Self-glory in the personal sphere and power for power's sake in the political sphere become our final guiding motives. Mayhem ensues.

Slaying Narcissus and Kratos

"Relativism" is a name for this attempt to slay beauty, truth, love, and justice. It comes in two forms. If we follow Narcissus, then the self—the autonomous individual—constructs reality for himself, herself, zirself, hirself, eirself, perssself, or themselves (including choosing which of those pronouns best fit one's sense of self, as kindly provided in chart form by federally funded organization Forge).[9] If we follow Kratos, then it is not the lone Me who gets to construct reality, but whatever collective We wins power.

There have been several devastating rebuttals to the individual relativism that says the almighty Me defines reality, as well as the cultural relativism that says the mightiest We defines reality.[10] I will not rehash those arguments here. Instead, I want to make a direct, unapologetic appeal to your humanity. Even if we have yet to meet, I care about you. I care about you being the most robust, fulfilled, and glorious version of yourself possible, the you with the gravitas and radiance that God designed you to reflect. That's my agenda. If you buy into the #youdoyou relativism of our age then, frankly, you are being conned out of three essential components of your truest self—courage, credibility, and Christ.

Courage: Relativism Makes Cowards of Us All

Relativism has a way of reducing our moral convictions to the level of our ice cream preferences. A lamenting Harvard graduate declared, "The freedom of our day is the freedom to devote ourselves to any values we please, on the mere condition that we do not believe them to be true." Sure, you think mint chocolate chip is the best flavor, but don't oppress all the rainbow sorbeteers, rocky roaders, and mocha almond fudgers of the world. *The* Truth is an illusion; everyone has *their* truth.

It is helpful here to ponder the difference between lowercase-*t* truths and uppercase-*T* Truth. For me, it is true with a lowercase *t* that Hattie B's is the best hot chicken joint in downtown Nashville. Would I die for that belief? Of course not. If someone said, "No, Prince's Hot Chicken Shack serves up a far better bird!" I might as well shrug my shoulders and say, "That may be true for you, but not for me." Some "truths" merit the lowercase *t* because they really are just personal opinions.

Contrary to relativism, there is also such a thing as a capital-*T* Truth. We detect it in the words of escaped slave and great American abolitionist Frederick Douglass: "I love the pure, peaceable, and impartial Christianity of Christ: I therefore hate the corrupt, slaveholding, women-whipping, cradle-plundering, partial and hypocritical Christianity of this land.... The slave auctioneer's bell and the church-going bell chime in with each other, and the bitter cries of the heartbroken slave are drowned in the religious shouts of his pious master."[11]

That is not the way relativists talk. Instead, they pontificate about "coexisting and equally valid patterns of life which mankind has created for itself."[12] When confronted with those who steal men, whip women, and rob cradles, Douglass did not stoop to mealy-mouthed clichés about "equally valid patterns of life." He would have none of the nonsense of cultural relativism.[13] (Iranian human rights activist Shirin Ebadi defined cultural relativism best as "nothing but an excuse to violate human rights."[14]) Douglass courageously exposed the evils of the "Christianity of this land" because he held the dominant culture to a standard higher than culture itself, what he called the "Christianity of Christ."[15]

Douglass looked to an authority above himself rather than grandstanding his own emotions as authoritative. He describes himself in the final line of his narrative as "faithfully relying upon the power of Truth, Love, and Justice, for success in my humble efforts—and solemnly pledging myself anew to the sacred cause."[16] Like Titian's lute player, Douglass looked to something bigger and beyond himself.

When Sophie Scholl and her White Rose Society exposed Hitler's Third Reich as "a dictatorship of evil"[17] and "an imperialist ideology of force . . . that must be shattered for all time,"[18] they too did not merely look inside for answers and live their truths. They believed in real universal good and evil. The great British abolitionist William Wilberforce had strong words for those, especially Christians, who say, "It doesn't matter what you believe, as long as you are sincere in your belief." Wilberforce bristled, "How absurd!"[19] With the help of the Clapham Sect and other nonrelativist allies, he went on to topple the "enormous . . . dreadful. . . . wickedness of the slave trade."[20]

Again, those who champion relativistic #youdoyou ideologies don't talk like that. Given their worldview, they *cannot* talk like that without committing logical suicide.[21] Their pep talks of self-affirmation are to the words of the great justice-seekers what the sounds of taco-induced flatulence are to a Beethoven sonata. Our generation needs a hundred million more courageous Douglasses, Scholls, and Wilberforces, brave souls calling us to the Truth above us.[22]

> Our generation needs a hundred million more courageous Douglasses, Scholls, and Wilberforces.

If relativism is true, however (a contradiction unto itself), then who could fault the slave traders or the Gestapo for being their true selves? Sartre is right that "everything is permissible if God does not exist"[23] because "we are on a plane where there are only men."[24] If there's nothing beyond this world, then it is impossible to work for a better world, since "better" implies a standard above this world to progress toward. Relativists, therefore, could never have, in good faith, interlocked arms with the Selma marchers, forged the secret bonds of Sophie

Scholl's White Rose Society, or unified the Velvet Revolutionaries to drive the Communists out of Czechoslovakia. In sum, relativism robs us of courage.

Credibility: Relativism Makes Hypocrites of Us All

Relativism also costs us our credibility. I had a window seat on a 737 headed for Birmingham from LAX. I sat, trying my best to decipher my Greek New Testament. The woman next to me—we'll call her "Mimi"—took notice and announced to her friend on her cell phone, "I've gotta go! The guy next to me is reading a Bible. Can you believe it? This is going to be a fun flight!" Mimi ended the call and aired her gripes against Christianity. I sat and listened as her arguments seemed to be reaching a crescendo. Then they did. "I guess what drives me most crazy about Christians is that they have the arrogance to believe they are right and everyone else is wrong. I mean that's just so *wrong* of them!"

I repeated Mimi's point back to her, hoping she might catch the irony. "It sounds like you have a problem with Christians believing that other people are wrong, and you believe that is— what was your word for it again?—*wrong* of them." "Exactly," she confirmed. Shoulders of other passengers began bouncing up and down as they tried to stifle laughter. I tried again. "You're calling millions of Christians wrong for thinking millions of other people are wrong?" "Yes," she replied, "I mean how could they be so self-righteous and . . ." She caught herself. At last came the aha moment. "Ohhh," Mimi said, and God bless her for her honest admission that she herself was guilty of committing against Christians the very transgression she loathed them for committing. What followed was a lively conversation as Mimi and I sat in the sky, forty thousand feet over the jagged green, beige, and auburn patchwork of middle America.

The moral of the story is that no one is quite the tolerant relativist they think they are. Even championing tolerance as a moral ideal for all people in all times should be enough to have one's credentials as a relativist revoked. We're all moral absolutists deep down if we believe that human beings should be treated with dignity and respect.

When I taught ethics at a secular college, I would ask, "How many of you believe there is something wrong with America that could be changed for the better?" Inevitably, every hand

> No one is quite the tolerant relativist they think they are.

rose. I would wipe my brow and let out a melodramatic, "Phew! Thank God, none of you are moral relativists!" A true relativist is the stuff of myth, elusive like a yeti or leprechaun. Nietzsche was anything but relativistic in his stand against German nationalism and anti-Semitism. Sartre was anything but relativistic in his opposition to the "race murder" the French colonialists unleashed in Algeria. Pop superstars Madonna, Britney Spears, and Christina Aguilera sang, "We are bored with the concept of right and wrong," shortly after kissing one another during a "Like a Virgin/Hollywood" medley at the 2003 MTV awards. The concept of right and wrong becomes less boring to them when trolls slander them, their melodies are plagiarized, or they receive death threats from psychotic strangers. Suddenly, the biblical Ten Commandments—with their bans on lying, stealing, and murder—become far more interesting.

It's easy to be relativists when it suits us, especially if we hate conflict. But the second that someone cuts us off on the freeway, cuts the queue in front of us, hacks our online identity, breaks into our car, slanders us behind our back, or takes too long delivering our order, all our sanctimonious slogans about not passing judgment and others living their truths evaporate instantly in the heat of our moral indignation.

I've met plenty of self-professing relativists over the years. I've never met an *actual* relativist, and neither have you. If you think you meet a true specimen, you might kick them square in the shin, or reach for their purse or wallet, and see how long their relativism holds up in real life. As a Christian, of course, I can't condone such tactics. Instead, simply ask folks their view on Donald Trump or abortion or Islam. You will discover that the line has never been between moral absolutists and moral relativists; it is between moral absolutists honest about what they are and moral absolutists pretending to be what they are not.

Christ: Relativism Reduces Jesus to Dr. Phil

Relativism robs you of courage and credibility. But it also attempts to pry something infinitely more precious away from you. If relativism is true, then good and evil are nothing more than human constructs. If there is no uppercase-*G* Good or uppercase-*E* Evil, then Jesus can't really be an uppercase-*S* Savior. In the relativist's lowercase world, Jesus can't change you from depraved to saved, but only help you achieve your personal dreams, like a sappy, self-help guru.

This kind of high-fiving, way-to-go-tiger life-coach Jesus is light-years away from the actual absolutist Jesus. Jesus did not come to validate and celebrate our every feeling and whim; he loves us far too much to do that. The actual Jesus made his own mission clear:

- Jesus said he came to "proclaim good news to the poor" (Luke 4:18), which makes sense only if there is such a thing as "good."
- Jesus said, "The Son of Man came to seek and to save the

lost" (Luke 19:10), a waste of time if there is no destination beyond our own subjective wanderings.

- Jesus said he came to do "the will of him who sent me" (John 6:38), an impossible mission if human wills are the supreme standards of morality and meaning.
- Jesus said, "For judgment I came into this world" (John 9:39), a clear violation of the relativist's dictum to never judge.
- Jesus said, "For this purpose I was born and for this purpose I have come into the world—to bear witness to the truth" (John 18:37), a pointless mission if there is no such thing as *the* truth, only your truth and my truth.
- Paul said, "Christ Jesus came into the world to save sinners" (1 Tim. 1:15), a fool's errand if sin is just a human construct.

Jesus came to love, forgive, save, redeem, and transform you, not validate, excuse, placate, stagnate, and flatter you. He never calls you to affirm yourself and follow your heart, but to deny yourself and follow him. Don't settle for the pushover Christ that #youdoyou relativism requires. Like Titian's lute player, find true inspiration by looking outside yourself. Look to him. He is the real-world Venus, Veritas, Cupid, and Themis. Christ *is* beauty, truth, love, and justice. The Jesus who exists outside your imagination— the one who poured his creative genius into making the universe, the one born in real human flesh in real time-space history, who morally triumphed in all the areas where we fail, who became our perfect substitute on the cross, who rose bodily from the dead, not as a ghost, hologram, or inspirational idea, who ascended and sits enthroned over his cosmos, the one you have to thank for the breath in your lungs and pulse in your veins—*that* Jesus has more saving power than you or I could possibly imagine. Ask him for some.

A Heretic's Testimonial

Josh McDowell has written or cowritten over 150 books that have been translated into 128 languages and has shared evidence for the truth of Christianity with millions of people in 139 countries and over 1,200 universities. Most of all, he is a devoted family man who loves Jesus. He is also a heretic to the cult of self-worship. He boldly breaks the #youdoyou commandment. This is his story.

I had a dysfunctional family life: an alcoholic and violent father, a depressed and obese mom, and Wayne, our farmhand who began sexually molesting me at age six. Any time my mom was gone, Wayne came looking for me. Twice I told her about it, but she refused to believe me. I was devastated.

This left me with emotional scars, bitterness, and a deep shame that made me want to die. I remember thinking, "There is no love in the world. No purpose. No God." When I was eleven, I actually cursed God. No one in my family ever showed me physical affection, not even my mom. Instead of feeling love, I felt rage. I don't know who I hated more, my dad, Wayne, or God.

When my dad drank, he got mean. He nearly killed my mom several times by beating her. Some days I'd try to get even, tying him up in our barn for hours. As Mom lay covered in blood and sometimes barn manure, she defended his violence. I'm convinced she died of a broken heart.

When I entered college, I took great pleasure in mocking the Christians on campus with their silly moral absolutes.

One day some of them challenged me to disprove Jesus Christ's resurrection. I accepted. As a prelaw student, I knew how to research. I decided to refute the resurrection by proving the Bible to be historically unreliable. That summer I studied the writings of notable skeptics in prestigious museums and libraries across Europe. To be intellectually fair, I also studied the writings of skeptics who became Christians in spite of their skepticism. I wasn't pleased that every piece of evidence I could find pointed to one conclusion: the Bible does accurately record real events, including Christ's ministry, crucifixion, and resurrection.

I realized that if the resurrection actually happened, then God was real. I couldn't ignore the facts. I found it hard to sleep at night, and my grades suffered. So I visited a local pastor, Pastor Logan, whose sermons I had often challenged. This particular evening, his words got my attention. Beads of sweat formed on my forehead as he outlined the steps of accepting Jesus as Savior. I wanted to trust God, but that seemed to require a big leap of faith. I was afraid my friends would say I was committing intellectual suicide. Then I felt God overwhelm me with a sense of his undeniable love. I made a heartfelt decision to trust Christ.

God began working on my hate by helping me forgive my dad. Several months later I told him, "Dad, I love you," and I meant it. That's when I knew Christianity was real! Next, I needed to forgive Wayne. I thought this would be impossible, but I made the agonizing choice to go forward. When Wayne opened his door, I blurted out, "Christ died for you, Wayne, as much as he died for me. So, I forgive you." A peace I'd never experienced before filled me.

Inconceivably, God used me to lead my dad to Christ. I was rear-ended by a drunk driver and had to lay flat on my back for weeks. Upon arriving home from the hospital, I expected my dad to be drunk. But he was sober. Dad was crying. He leaned over me, his tears dripping onto my face. "Son, how can you love a father like me?" I choked back my tears. "Because Jesus loves you, Dad, and he wants a relationship with you." "If Jesus can do in my life what I've seen him do in yours," he replied, "then I want to know him."

After Dad's humble prayer, God supernaturally removed his thirty-year addiction to alcohol. His transformation was so dramatic that many in our hometown decided to follow Christ! I used to think I was damaged goods. But God always had a plan to use my intellectual curiosity and my pain for his glory. He can do the same for you. It is not a matter of #youdoyou, it is a matter of Jesus redeeming you.

—Josh

A Heretic's Prayer

Dear God,
You exist and you are the standard of beauty, truth, love, and justice. Like Titian's lute player, may we look beyond ourselves for ultimate answers. May we look to you and your Word.
As we look above rather than within, please make us more courageous, more credible, and more Christ-centered. And as our culture frowns on the very notion of sin, help us to love people enough to risk the momentary social discomfort to

openly invite people to repentance and faith in Jesus, not as a way, but as the way to salvation. And help us to live that truth, living out the supreme Lordship of Jesus over every square inch of our lives. Amen.

A Heretic's Field Manual

Before moving on to the next chapter, do at least three of the following to sharpen your skills at violating the #youdoyou commandment:

1. Judges 21:25 recounts the days in which "there was no king in Israel [and] everyone did what was right in his own eyes." Peruse the closing chapters of Judges, and ask what kind of havoc people unleash when they do what is right in their own eyes. Then ask the same question of our day.
2. Walk in nature for about twenty minutes. Try to count how many beauties you do not invent but discover. Ponder not *what* but *who* the source of that beauty is.
3. Ours is a world of unrisky, air-conditioned, latte-sipping, virtue-signaling pursuits of justice. What is something you could do, not in cyberspace but in real life, to help people in your daily orbit? Go do that thing.
4. Ask God if he is calling you to positively impact a particularly broken aspect of the world. Pray with an honest willingness, making yourself fully available to step in wherever he calls you.
5. Think about the culture you are in, the waters you swim

in daily. Consider the parts of culture that are out of whack with God's perspective on human flourishing. See if you can think of three ways Jesus's vision is superior to your culture's vision. Try to pinpoint one thing you can do today to be countercultural in a Christ-exalting way.

Chapter 6

#yolo

Thou shalt pursue the rush of boundary-free experience.

It seems as though a new society was arising which will acknowledge no hierarchy of values, no intellectual authority and no social or religious tradition, but which will live for the moment in a chaos of pure sensation.
—CHRISTOPHER DAWSON, BRITISH PHILOSOPHER

[Our] task on earth . . . cannot be unrestrained enjoyment of everyday life. . . . It has to be the fulfillment of a permanent, earnest duty so that one's life journey may become an experience of moral growth, so that one may leave life a better human being than one started it. . . . The human soul longs for things higher, warmer, and purer than those offered by today's mass living habits.
—ALEKSANDR SOLZHENITSYN, RUSSIAN NOVELIST

We have seen that self-glorification robs us of awe. It makes us hypertraditionalists by forcing us to abide by the dogmas of an ancient serpent. It dupes us into following our own dull, dithering, divided, depraved, and delusional hearts. It lures us, like obedient cows, to unsavory ideologues who care nothing for our good. It leads to a relativism that costs us our courage, credibility, and Christ. Any one of those arguments should be enough to pull us from the abyss of self-centered living. But there are more. Self-worship promises a tingly rush of adventure and the buzz of unfettered experience, often advertised with the slogan #yolo (You only live once).[1]

The Great Flattening

The yolo acronym was first trademarked in 1993 by a small sports gear company, became the name of the Grateful Dead drummer's Sonoma ranch in 1996, and got national airplay for the first time in 2004 on a reality show called *Average Joe*. But the acronym took off when hip-hop megastar Drake used it in the hook of his 2011 hit "The Motto." Yolo swept the nation from 2012–2013 but became increasingly cringy when anyone over twenty-five used it. Today it is used either sarcastically or by out-of-touch youth leaders feigning relevance. In its heyday, yolo did the work that phrases like "seize the day" (*carpe diem*) did for earlier generations, but STD does not have quite the same appeal as YOLO, for obvious reasons.

Though the word has lost its cool factor, the attitude toward life it captured is alive and well, and, in a sense, always will be. On some level, all of us long for adventures, with all their unpredictability, adrenaline rushes, and hope. As Gandalf the Grey put it, "It's a dangerous business, Frodo, going out your door. You step onto the road, and if you don't keep your feet, there's no knowing where you might be swept off to."

Some express their longing to be swept off in adventure by jet-setting to exotic destinations. Others brandish jerseys and tribal face paint to join their favorite sports franchise on their seasonal quest for the World Series, Stanley Cup, or Super Bowl. Others express it by sitting on their couches, chests speckled with potato chip shrapnel, living vicarious adventures through their favorite television heroes. Video games scratch the same itch for many, empowering us to become Italian plumbers saving the princess from the evil Bowser, *Call of Duty* soldiers sniping Nazis, or busty elf goddesses slaying mutant dragons. We long for grand stories, and we long to be characters who make meaningful differences in those stories.

As a kid I spent hours in my backyard with a bow and arrow, pretending I was Robin Hood with his band of merry men rebelling against the tyranny of evil Prince John. The next day I might be Luke Skywalker deflecting imaginary pew pews with my plastic saber, taking on the Empire. How many kids with sticks pretend they're joining Dumbledore's army to battle "he who must not be named"?

This raises a problem for the self-worshiper. If I am the sovereign maker of my own morality, then I'm just like everyone else, gods unto themselves manufacturing their own moralities. Who, then, can fault Prince John, Emperor Palpatine, or Lord Voldemort for being their true selves? Under the dogma of self-worship, we might as well disband the merry men, cancel the Rebellion, and close Hogwarts.

All the great adventures unfold on excitingly layered moral terrain. Self-worship levels this terrain to rubble. Real adventures have pinnacles of glory to aspire to—a free Middle-earth, Aslan's country, a galaxy far, far away liberated from the Empire, a world where the magical and the Muggle peacefully coexist without genocidal wizards or joy-sucking dementors spoiling it for everyone. There are real valleys of danger and despair. There are real villains, real trials and temptations, real virtues to acquire and vices to shed. Self-worship makes all of that impossible.

Recall the defining moment in the film adaptation of Tolkien's *The Two Towers* where we eavesdrop on Frodo and Sam atop the battle-torn ruins of Osgiliath. Frodo is exhausted and hopeless.

> **Frodo:** What are we holding on to, Sam?
> **Sam:** That there's some good in this world, Mr. Frodo, and it's worth fighting for.

Sam has just articulated an essential ingredient of all true adventures—goodness in the world worth fighting for. Now imagine a self-worshiper's cut of the same scene:

> **Frodo:** What are we holding on to, Sam?
> **Sam:** That there is no transcendent goodness in this world, Mr. Frodo, only your subjective projections of goodness into a cosmic void in which our mission to Mordor is no better, in any deep sense, than Sauron's mission to get his ring back or the Uruk-hai's mission to get man-flesh back on the menu.

Making ourselves the standard of goodness sucks all true adventure out of life. Adventurers need old travelers who have journeyed farther and have hard-won wisdom to pass on. Self-worshipers, by contrast, need no Gandalf, Obi-Wan, or Dumbledore to commission and guide their efforts. They need only their own impulses. Self-worship becomes a gigantic steam roller that flattens all of life to one never-ending plateau—no peaks to climb, no valleys to brave, no jagged terrain to heave our tired selves over in the pursuit of some high and noble goal.

Why does self-worship make the earth so flat? If you are the standard of your own meaning and morality, then there is nothing above you to aspire toward. The word "upward" carries no meaning. At any given moment, you are the high point, the pinnacle, your own north star, your own happily ever after. If that's the case, then you could no more make objective moral progress—the kind Aragorn and Arwen, Harry and Hermione, and Luke and Leia make—than a man can pull the scruff of his own neck to lift his feet off the ground. You could never, in any deep sense, become a *better* version of yourself, only a *different* version of yourself. Making yourself supreme means you can never venture vertically, only horizontally, never upward, only sideways toward equally flat horizons. How dull.

> If you yourself are the standard of your own meaning and morality, then there is nothing above you to aspire toward.

Further or Further Up?

This sideways attempt at adventure is captured well in Tom Wolfe's 1968 book *The Electric Kool-Aid Acid Test*. Wolfe provides a nonfiction chronicle of a quasi–cult leader and countercultural icon named Ken Kesey on an LSD-fueled cross-country bus trip with his group of "Merry Pranksters." The bus is painted in a psychedelic array of primary colors with a destination placard that didn't name a city but simply read "Further." Wolfe documents the Merry Pranksters attempts to go not only geographically farther—from California to New York—but further into human consciousness. Hence, the copious amounts of LSD, speed, and pot. They host

"Acid Tests" around the country, with acid-infused Kool-Aid, along with dancing, light shows, and live music (often courtesy of the Grateful Dead) to enhance everyone's trip.

Fleeing charges of marijuana possession, the Pranksters end up in Mexico, where their acid trips start losing their potency. They eventually return to the United States, where Kesey, now a counterculture celebrity, gets arrested. The authorities briefly release him to host an "Acid Test Graduation" to prove that he and his followers could achieve higher consciousness without mind-altering drugs. After the uneventful evening, Kesey was sentenced to a work camp.

The Electric Kool-Aid Acid Test offers what we might call a hopelessly sideways adventure, which, therefore, ceases to be a true adventure. The Merry Pranksters begin only with their finite selves and, therefore, end only with their finite selves. Without God, they could only go further, never further *upward*.

Contrast this with Frodo and Sam, who climb *up* the sharp igneous lava rocks of Mount Doom to set Middle-Earth free. Neo and Trinity careen *up* in the Logos ship to the Machine City to deliver Zion. Iron Man flies *up* through a portal in the sky to hurl a nuke at the Chitauri mothership and save New York. Contrast the merely further tale of Kesey and his Merry Pranksters with the further *up* experience of the adventurers in C. S. Lewis's Chronicles of Narnia series. In the final pages of *The Last Battle*, we read, "They went through winding valley after winding valley and up the steep sides of hills and, faster than ever, down the other side, following the river and sometimes crossing it and skimming across mountain lakes as if they were living speedboats. . . . 'Further up and further in!' roared the Unicorn, and no one held back."[2]

The adventurers eventually rise to enter the golden gates of Aslan's country, where Lucy's first Narnian friend, Tumnus the Faun, tells her, "The further up and the further in you go, the bigger everything gets." "I see," Lucy responds, "This is still Narnia, and more real and more beautiful than the Narnia below."[3] Then Lewis closes his seven-book saga: "We can most truly say that they lived happily ever after. But for them it was only the beginning of the real story. All their life in this world and all their adventures in Narnia had only been the cover and the title page: now at last they were beginning Chapter One of the Great Story which no one on earth has read: which goes on forever: in which every chapter is better than the one before."[4]

The self-worshiper's doctrine of #yolo steals "up" and "happily ever after" from our vocabulary. There is only further, never further *up*. There is nothing above the self, only a long sideways series of rushes that fry our neurons, scar our livers, sear our consciences, and thrash our families.

Compared with real upward adventures, #yolo means something else entirely. "You only live once" reduces us to a godless and, therefore, flat universe. You live on a dying planet in a solar system with its own impending expiration date within the expanding universe headed for heat death.[5] No truth exists beyond your own feelings, no goodness you don't invent, no beauty beyond your own retinas, nothing to protect from vandals, nothing worth living and dying for. You wander cyberspace, a digital domain crafted by profit-seeking corporations to maximize dopamine hits to your tired amygdala.

If you follow the #yolo dogma to say yes to bungee-jumping, rock-climbing, skinny-dipping, acid-dropping, or other forms of thrill-seeking, then the rushes wear off. If you find the sweet buzz of infatuation or love, under the dogmas of self-worship, you will move on when your lovers fail to deliver on your God-sized expectations of fulfillment. If you dabble with transcendental meditation, magic crystals, or whatever other Eastern trend is sweeping the West, you end up, like a junkie, chasing elusive highs. Deep down, an existential dread haunts you, the terrible sense that you're somehow missing out on what life has to offer. You slowly become as vacant as the aged Tim Leary, as "gaga" as Jean-Paul Sartre, or as imprisoned as Ken Kesey. Then you die and become worm food. After all, you only live once.

He baptizes the mundane with meaning.

#Yolo loses its pull as the electrifying call of romantics, bohemians, and thrill-seekers. It becomes instead the defeated sigh of someone who wasted their years chasing a mountaintop high that the flatlands of self-worship could never provide.

The Grand Adventure

Thankfully, you don't only live once. None of us does. Each of us is an everlasting being. As C. S. Lewis put it, "You have never talked to a mere mortal. Nations, cultures, arts, civilizations—these are mortal, and their life is to ours as the life of a gnat."[6] Like it or not, you will last forever. Eternity is built into your design.

The same Creator who put eternity in our hearts invites us into an adventure of cosmic proportions. "For the weapons of our warfare are not of the flesh but have divine power to destroy strongholds" (2 Cor. 10:4). "For we do not wrestle against flesh and blood, but against the rulers, against the authorities, against the cosmic powers over this present darkness, against the spiritual forces of evil in the heavenly places" (Eph. 6:12). We are invited to join the resurrected Jesus—the snake slayer, the Lion of Judah, the crucified Lamb who defeated death—in his mission to proclaim the good news to the ends of the earth. We are commissioned to participate in his global rescue mission to transfer people from the dominion of darkness into his kingdom of light (Col. 1:13). We are called to shine like lights in a crooked and twisted generation (Phil. 2:15), to overcome evil with good (Rom. 12:21) until the God of peace crushes history's archvillain—Satan—under our feet (Rom. 16:20).

Where does this real-life adventure end? The Bible tells us no mind has conceived what God has in store for us (1 Cor. 2:9). Whatever happy ending God has planned for you is better than your wildest dreams and certainly better than anything you could achieve by living your life by a hashtag that corporations use to hawk bracelets and athletic shoes.

A Closing Word on the Mundane

You may feel your pulse quicken at the prospect of an adventurous Christ-centered life. The adventure to which God calls us, though, does not mean you will swing on vines across the piranha-infested Amazon, kicking anacondas in the face and dodging poison blow darts to bring the first-ever translated Bible to a remote tribe.

Even the greatest adventures have mundane moments. The eleven hours and twenty minutes of the *Lord of the Rings* film trilogy would have lasted years if Peter Jackson had decided to include every time the heroes took a nap, talked about nothing in particular, waited for the taters to boil, or snuck off into the forest to relieve themselves. Jesus—the theanthropos (the God-man), the star of the greatest adventure of history—hammered busted chairs, cooked breakfast, napped, and sweat in the Middle Eastern sun. Few of Jesus's mundane tasks made it into the four gospels.

In John 8:29 Jesus says he *always* does what pleases the Father. That includes the little things. The Christian life—the greatest adventure we can aspire to—is composed of a million seemingly small, cross-shaped acts. When Jesus separates the sheep from the goats (Matt. 25), he does not make some magnanimous, earth-shaking feat the defining mark of his sheep. No. Cold water for the thirsty, a coat for the chilly, a visit to the lonesome—these are the marks of Jesus's followers.

The adventure to which God calls us in Scripture is nothing

like a round-the-clock acid trip.[7] If we market following Jesus that way, then we aren't marketing the actual Jesus, but Ken Kesey dressed in a white robe with a fake beard offering another trip. The adventure Jesus calls us to is far better. He does not turn us into junkies always trying to escape the humdrum realities of everyday life. Rather, he died bodily and rose bodily to redeem whole people, body and soul. He doesn't whisk us away from the world. He enters our everyday lives. He baptizes the mundane with meaning, even if we can't always detect it. He pushes back the forces of darkness as we tell a neighbor about him despite the social risk, as we move furniture, change diapers, scrub dishes, take the insult, greet the awkward outsider, crack the well-timed joke in the stuffy room, or treat the waiter like more than a means to the end of our tacos.

We embark on an adventure with eternal stakes by doing what David Foster Wallace called "sacrificing for [others] over and over, in myriad petty little unsexy ways."[8] By preaching the gospel with our words and embodying it in our daily actions, we toss the ring into Mount Doom, fire the proton torpedo into the Death Star exhaust port, destroy the Horcruxes. Daily life takes on eternal significance. Because we are eternal beings, we can join the *real* adventure that lasts forever.

A Heretic's Testimonial

Alyssa Poblete is a writer and a church planter in Rancho Santa Margarita, California, with her husband, Chris, and their three children. She is also a heretic to the cult of self-worship. She boldly breaks the #yolo commandment. This is her story.

The number is 2,866. That is how many days in a row I have changed a diaper over the last seven years. The twenty-three-year-old version of myself had a heart swirling with aspirations, none of which included daily diaper duty. The thing about diapers is, they are always there, tethering my days around a ritual that is unavoidable and constant. The work of diapering is a liturgy of sorts, demanding my attention (often at the most inopportune moments). It slows me down, creates detours and obstacles to my days, and relentlessly refuses to fit into a neatly formed schedule.

Even more than that, the work is utterly mundane—or worse, lamentable. I've been known to shed a tear or two over the matter (like the time one of my children peed in my face while I was breastfeeding another, or when our son tried to change his own diaper—his crib looked like a scene from a horror film). Those big dreams of a life filled with meaning and significance bubble to the surface at times as I take out one more bag of trash and confront yet another potty training pooptastrophe. If this is all there is, how unremarkable. And truthfully, if #yolo is the mantra of my days, then, yes, this is somewhat of an unfortunate tale. But the work is there every day, and it's necessary work. As the saying goes, everyone wants a revolution but nobody wants to do the dishes.

In Christ, ordinary work mingles with the extraordinary. In all the menial tasks, we find ourselves thrust into an epic story with eternal implications. Diapering and other seemingly pointless daily tasks matter in God's economy. However small the investment may seem, it is an advancement in God's kingdom purposes. Even Mary had to wipe the rear of a baby that would one day change the world.

If I live my days to be limitless and unbound by the banal tasks of life, I will miss the extraordinary implications of the work right before me. I will miss the budding heart of someone whose first memories will be as a recipient of love and grace. I will miss the joy of witnessing a child becoming more readily inclined to love God because of a thousand tiny acts that created a culture of sacrifice and love. In all those unseen moments, I will miss the huge, kingdom implications of this unremarkable work—that the changing of a diaper might help change a heart, and a changed heart might change the world. May we make the most of our days in the millions of tiny acts that make an epic difference for time and eternity.

—Alyssa

A Heretic's Prayer

God,
You call us above ourselves to demolish evil strongholds,
wrestle the cosmic powers of this present darkness, overcome
evil with good, declare the gospel of life to the nations, and
crush Satan under our feet. That is far more adventurous
than looking inside ourselves. Help us, even today, to be more
attuned to the cosmic battle happening in our midst. Help us
resist vice and grow in Christlike virtue. Give us an extra dose
of supernatural endurance in the long valleys. Help us to stay
faithful on the tumbleweeded plains of life. And may you get
all the glory when we are on the peaks. May the good news of
Jesus's death and resurrection permeate our entire lives. May

we live consistently with the fact that we don't only live once.
Help us to live in the light of eternity. Amen.

A Heretic's Field Manual

Before moving on to the next chapter, do three or four of the following to sharpen your skills at violating the #yolo commandment:

1. The reality of cosmic evil forces warring against God's glory and our joy is severely underestimated today. Spend five minutes praying that God—by the power of the finished cross-work and resurrection of Jesus—would sovereignly sabotage whatever forces of darkness may be attacking you or your loved ones.
2. Think of three things you can do to sacrifice for others today. Go do those things.
3. Your participation in God's redemptive mission has everything to do with your new identity "in Christ." Take a few minutes in solitude to commune with him. Thank Jesus for his perfection that became yours through the cross and for the wrath he bore on your behalf. Praise him for rising from the dead to make your life eternally significant.
4. To press into the unpredictability of following Christ, give more money or time than you can afford to someone in need.
5. Ask God for clarity on your specific role in his cosmic defeat of evil. Make yourself utterly available to embark on that adventure.

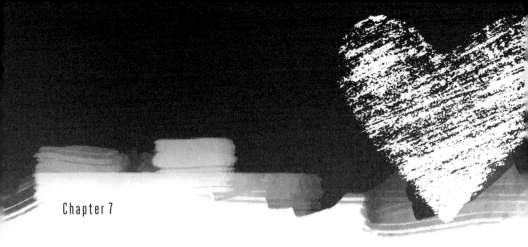

Chapter 7

#theanswersarewithin

Thou shalt trust yourself, never letting anyone oppress you with the antiquated notion of being a "sinner."

The heart wants what it wants.
—WOODY ALLEN, FILMMAKER (TRYING TO EXPLAIN HIS AFFAIR
WITH THE YOUNG DAUGHTER OF MIA FARROW)

Like a neurotic little god, the human heart keeps ending discussions by insisting that it wants what it wants.
—CORNELIUS PLANTINGA, SYSTEMATIC THEOLOGIAN

At twenty-one-years-old, pop sensation Christina Aguilera wrote "The Voice Within," a piano-driven ballad that topped charts in several countries. "Look inside yourself. . . . Just trust the voice within," she sang. Critics hailed the tune as "breathtaking," "inspired," and "powerful." "It basically reduces us to tears every time we hear it,"[1] said Rachel McRady of *Wetpaint*. If you attempted to live out the lyrics of this hit, then, indeed, you should be in tears, but not for the same reasons as McRady.

To see the tragedy in what was meant to be an inspirational ballad, consider the *New York Times* bestseller *The Coddling of the American Mind* by Greg Lukianoff and Jonathan Haidt. They chronicle nine of the most common cognitive distortions that occur within us. Mentally check off how many of them you have fallen for:

1. **Emotional reasoning:** Letting your feelings guide your interpretation of reality.
2. **Catastrophizing:** Focusing on the worst possible outcome.
3. **Overgeneralizing:** Perceiving a global pattern of negatives based on a single incident.
4. **Dichotomous thinking:** Viewing people or events in all-or-nothing terms.
5. **Mind reading:** Assuming you know what people think without having sufficient evidence of their thoughts.
6. **Labeling:** Assigning global negative traits to yourself or others.

7. **Negative filtering:** Focusing almost exclusively on the negatives and seldom noticing the positives.
8. **Discounting positives:** Claiming that the positive things you or others do are trivial.
9. **Blaming:** Focusing on the other person as the *source* of your negative feelings; you refuse to take responsibility for changing yourself.[2]

I have practiced all nine. (Some I have practiced so much I'm practically a virtuoso.) Try to pinpoint the two or three distortions you are most susceptible to.

There is encouraging news. All nine cognitive distortions can be largely stripped of their destructive power over our minds. But if we decide to look within for answers, then we turn ourselves in the exact opposite direction from the tried and tested roads to restoration and healing.

Cognitive behavioral therapy (or CBT), pioneered by psychiatrist Aaron Beck in the 1960s, has become a go-to method in the world of therapy. There is overwhelming evidence of its effectiveness in combating not only depression and anxiety but also anorexia, bulimia, obsessive compulsive disorder, anger, marital discord, and stress-related disorders.[3] What is CBT? I offer a simple definition:

Cognitive behavioral therapy (noun): The exact opposite of following our hearts and looking within for answers.

CBT tells us to challenge our hearts. Question our feelings. Deliberately debunk negative emotions and replace them with better emotions. Humbly recognize that there are truths higher than our hearts. Strive to align our hearts with reality rather than distort reality to match our jumbled feelings.

If we follow pop ethicist Christina Aguilera, telling us to "just trust the voice within," what do we do when that voice tells us, "The sky is falling—panic!" or, "Things will just go from bad to worse—despair!"? What happens when the voice within clamors with catastrophic thinking, overgeneralizing, negative filtering, and blaming?

Ancient Jewish CBT

Cognitive behavioral therapy is another case of science gradually catching up to the Scriptures. Psalm 42 is a prime example of biblical CBT from nearly three thousand years before Aaron Beck published his discoveries and altered the landscape of modern psychotherapy. The psalmist looks within, and what he finds is not pretty. He's been crying day and night (v. 3), his soul is cast down (v. 5), he feels crushed by God's waves (v. 7), forgotten by his Creator, oppressed by his enemies (v. 9)—in a word, "turmoil" (v. 11). In Psalm 42, we can detect all nine of the cognitive distortions from Lukianoff and Haidt's list.

Then the ancient psalmist does something that is a mark of mental health. He argues with his feelings. "Why are you cast down, O my soul, and why are you in turmoil within me?" (v. 5).[4] He marshals three arguments against the cynicism within— arguments from the past, present, and future.

The psalmist recalls better days swept up in joyous worship procession at the Jerusalem temple (v. 4). He jogs his memory by naming specific places—Jordan, Hermon, and Mount Mizar (v. 6)— where he has encountered God's sustaining goodness. He finds that "my soul is cast down within me" (v. 6). Rather than plunge deeper *within*, the psalmist looks *up*. "Therefore I remember you" (v. 6). Turning to the present, the psalmist notices God's daily and nightly care. "By day the LORD commands his steadfast love, and at night his song is with me" (v. 8). With hopeful eyes toward the future based on God's proven character, he says, "Hope in God; for I shall again praise him, my salvation and my God" (v. 11).

As one comedian put it, "If [your heart] tells you to strangle kittens or something, then don't follow it anymore. I mean it's just a heart, right? It's not the Dalai Lama."[5] We could expand the punch line biblically. If your heart tells you that you are a pathetic, godforsaken waste of space, forever condemned to an everlasting dark night of the soul, then don't follow your heart anymore. Your emotions are not gospel truth. They aren't. Your heart is not Yahweh. What he says about you is infinitely more trustworthy and hopeful. God suffers from no cognitive distortions. Take him far more seriously than your own heart. God's Word will last forever; your depressing or anxious feelings won't.

> **God's Word will last forever; your depressing or anxious feelings won't.**

Practicing Biblical CBT Yourself

How might we practice biblical CBT instead of naively looking within for answers? Psalm 1 is enormously helpful here.

> Blessed is the man
>> who walks not in the counsel of the wicked,
> nor stands in the way of sinners,
>> nor sits in the seat of scoffers;
> but his delight is in the law of the LORD,
>> and on his law he meditates day and night.
>
> He is like a tree
>> planted by streams of water
> that yields its fruit in its season,
>> and its leaf does not wither.
> In all that he does, he prospers.
> The wicked are not so,
>> but are like chaff that the wind drives away.

> Therefore the wicked will not stand in the judgment,
>> nor sinners in the congregation of the righteous;
> for the LORD knows the way of the righteous,
>> but the way of the wicked will perish.

These six verses contain a brilliance that is lost on most twenty-first-century readers. Psalm 1 follows what scholars call "chiastic structure." The Greek letter *chi* is the same as our English letter *X*, so chiastic structure simply means a text is patterned in the shape of an X. This X-structure pops up again and again in the Bible. A text may begin with some idea A, followed by another idea B, then a third idea C. Then it reverses back on itself in the form of C'-B'-A', creating a kind of X shape. (In logic, the opposite of A is marked with an apostrophe as A'.)

Let's fill in the blanks with the chiastic structure of Psalm 1. The first word of the psalm is "blessed" (v. 1a), a plural in the Hebrew to express a life marked by exponentially multiplied fulfillment. The last word of the psalm is "perish" (v. 6), the opposite of "blessed" in the first verse. There's our A and A'. The second idea is how the blessed don't walk, stand, or sit with the wicked, sinners, and scoffers (v. 1b), while the second-to-last idea (v. 5) is that the perishing will not stand in the judgment or in the congregation of the righteous. There's our B and B'. The third big idea is a nature metaphor—the blessed are like deep-rooted fruitful trees (v. 3), followed by the third-to-last big idea, another nature metaphor—the perishing are like weightless, nutritionless chaff. And so we hit the middle of our X with our C and C'. For visual learners, it looks like this:

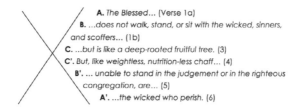

A. The Blessed... (Verse 1a)
B. ...does not walk, stand, or sit with the wicked, sinners, and scoffers... (1b)
C. ...but is like a deep-rooted fruitful tree. (3)
C'. But, like weightless, nutrition-less chaff... (4)
B'. ... unable to stand in the judgement or in the righteous congregation, are... (5)
A'. ...the wicked who perish. (6)

You may notice that something is off. Yes, the blessing of verse 1a and the perishing of verse 6 go together, the standing language of 1b and 5 go together, and the nature metaphors of 3 and 4 go together. But—and this is precisely the question the psalm was so ingeniously structured to evoke—*what about verse 2?* Something in the top half of the X has no corresponding part in the bottom half. The whole psalm is top-heavy. We find something in the top 3 verses that is missing in the bottom three verses. That watershed between the blessed and the perishing is found in the second verse:

> His delight is in the law of the LORD,
>> and on his law he meditates day and night.

Truly fulfilled and thriving people don't look within for answers. They find their joy in God's law and meditate on it often. The Hebrew for "meditates" here has nothing to do with sitting in lotus position, thumbs to index fingers, and chanting "omm." This is not the mind-emptying meditation of the East, but the mind-filling exercise of the ancient Jews. The root word means to mutter to oneself, chew like a cow chews its cud, and ponder what God says is true until his thoughts become our thoughts.

Picture your brain like a gigantic network of freeways. Some thought patterns are so frequently traveled that they have become superhighways with a dozen lanes in your brain matter. You send thoughts down the "I'm unlovable" superhighway. The longer you tell yourself such lies, the wider that superhighway becomes as more lanes are added to your neural pathways to accommodate the heavy traffic of self-doubt.

Here is how biblical meditation works. Open God's Word. Read, say, Jesus's prayer the night before his execution in John 17. He prays for everyone through the ages of time who would believe in him through the apostles' word. If you have placed your trust in him, then he is praying for *you*. In verse 23, he makes the staggering claim that the Father loves you *even as* he loves the Son. Ponder that for a few minutes and, in your headspace, some new ground is being cleared and steamrolled. Meditate longer. "The Father loves me *even as* he loves the Son. Wow!" Now the makings of a dirt road materialize, a small off-ramp from the self-loathing superhighway. Meditate some more. How does the Father love the Son within the Trinity? He loves the Son infinitely, unswervingly, unapologetically, with the full weight of his divine perfections. How then am I loved? The Father loves me infinitely, unswervingly, unapologetically, with the full weight of his divine perfections!

Dwell on that long enough and that old "I'm unlovable" superhighway gets less and less traffic. It falls into disrepair. Dust and shrubberies overtake it. Instead, you have a new superhighway in your head, the "I am loved even as the Father loves the Son" superhighway.

Slowly you think God's thoughts about yourself. What others think about you and even what you think about yourself matter less and less. Cognitive distortions no longer define you. Emotional reasoning, catastrophizing, overgeneralizing, dichotomous thinking, mind reading, labeling, negative filtering, discounting positives, and blaming become exceptions rather than rule your mental life.[6] You enter a new normal in which your default mode becomes thinking about "whatever is true, whatever is honorable, whatever is just, whatever is pure, whatever is lovely, whatever is commendable" (Phil. 4:8). Lo and behold, you become more truly yourself not by looking *within* for answers but by looking *up* for answers in God's Word.[7]

> You become more truly yourself not by looking *within* for answers but by looking *up* for answers.

Kill the Old Man

As if our cognitive distortions weren't enough to deter us from believing that #theanswersarewithin, there is more. We aren't brains in a vat or hearts on a stick. We aren't only cognitive and emotional beings, we are also *moral* beings. Our wills, just like our intellects and emotions, distort reality.[8] No conversation about looking within would be complete unless we reckon with the common moral distortions we fall for. Here are nine.

1. **Idolatry:** Making some finite thing the foundation of our identity.
2. **Pride:** Giving more reverence to ourselves than to God.
3. **Malevolence/resentment:** Harboring hatred and unforgiveness toward others.
4. **Lust/infidelity:** Looking at people as mere bodies to gratify our sexual drives and failing to honor the sacred marriage covenant.
5. **Deception:** Failing to keep our word, bending facts or outright fabricating facts in our own favor.
6. **Apathy/laziness:** Shrugging our shoulders at injustice, scrolling our minds into oblivion rather than working for the good of our neighbors.
7. **Over-indulgence:** Letting our appetites for food and drink control us rather than us controlling them.
8. **Theft:** Taking what doesn't belong to us.
9. **Greed/ungratefulness:** Hyperfocusing on what we don't have and hoarding what we do have.

Scripture has a word for the source of these moral distortions in our hearts. That word, in Greek, is *sarx*, translated as "flesh" or "sin nature." It is the New Testament label for the anti-God and, therefore, antilife drives within us that wage war against our souls (1 Peter 2:11; cf. James 4:1) and make us "captive to the law of sin" (Rom. 7:23). Sometimes Paul personifies the *sarx* as "the old self" (Eph. 4:22).

When we look within for answers, we find "the old self." He is a cutthroat fascist when it comes to seeking power, a hedonist shaking for the next fix when it comes to seeking pleasure, a shady defense attorney churning out cheap rationalizations for what we know is wrong, an egomaniac, a con artist, and an idolatrous, thieving, backstabbing, complaining, gluttonous pervert.

The answers-are-within folks often pretend such hell-bent characters within ourselves simply do not exist, or if they do, they exist only in other people. The self-serving bias is a powerful thing. We disguise these unflattering facets of our inner selves from public view. We hide them from ourselves. But no battle has ever been won by pretending the enemy doesn't exist, and a battle is precisely what the Christian life is. We are walking civil wars, Spirit versus flesh, with the God-seeking parts of us battling the God-shunning parts of us.

The Bible calls us to war: "Put on the armor of light. . . . [And] put on the Lord Jesus Christ, and make no provision for the flesh, to gratify its desires" (Rom. 13:12, 14). We must "crucify" our sin nature (Gal. 5:16–24). "For if you live according to the flesh you will die, but if by the Spirit you put to death the deeds of the body, you will live" (Rom. 8:13).[9]

Seven Phases along the Sin-Killing Continuum

The sin-killing that Paul describes happens along a continuum with seven phases. Try to figure out where you stand:

Phase 1: Sin is an old-fashioned superstition. I'm not at war against the *sarx*. Life by the sin nature does not lead to death.

Phase 2: The *sarx* does exist and leads to self-destruction. I need to do something about it. But the sin nature is a general, faceless problem.

Phase 3: Aha, I can see now what specific forms the *sarx* takes in my life. All I need is a few self-help measures to kill those sinful behaviors.

Phase 4: There is something way deeper going on here. My behavior modification isn't working. Underneath my sinful behaviors there must be sinful states in my heart that need to change.

Phase 5: My self-help efforts still aren't getting me anywhere. I'll take the sin in my heart's closet out into the light of community. I'll enlist trusted friends as allies in this battle.

Phase 6: I still haven't made my sin die. I need *supernatural* sin-killing power here. I will pray persistently, calling in the divine air support of the Holy Spirit to blast these internal evils to smithereens.

Phase 7: I have been prayerfully relying on God's power as I strive to kill sin, and sin is actually being killed. All praise and thanks to the sovereign God who changed my heart!

Which phase do you find yourself in? Wherever you are, move ahead. As John Owen reminds us, "Be killing sin or it will be killing you."[10] Don't let your sin drop bombs on your joy in God without blasting back with the supernatural power of the Holy Spirit. Don't look within for answers. Look above for answers, and call on the Holy Spirit.

A Heretic's Testimonial

Trevor Wright is a student of Scripture, fitness buff, loving husband, father, brother, and world-class beard grower. He is also a heretic to the cult of self-worship. He boldly breaks #theanswersarewithin commandment. This is his story.

Once every month or so, I weep silently as I fall asleep, feeling deeply alone. My wife, Sheryl, and I were married in 2015. Three years later we had one child, a second on the way, a stage IIIB colon cancer diagnosis, and a brutal, abusive ending to a ten-year church experience.

With emergency surgery and complete lifestyle change, I enjoyed two and a half years cancer free. The future was looking bright, and we were hopeful as we entered the infamous year: 2020. On December 23, 2020, I was diagnosed with stage IV colon cancer. Sheryl and I were expecting our third child just one month later. Doctors said I had a max of five to six years of life left, so I shifted my full focus to researching how to beat this and provide for my family.

Our sweet baby Jane was born January 11, 2021—our first girl! Five months later, she was diagnosed with a rare genetic condition. We were told it would significantly affect her growth. To this day it has not had any effect on her happiness. I'd pay top dollar to smile like baby Jane.

In those lonely, quiet moments before sleep, I remember that something is growing inside my body that threatens to take away everything I love. I want my family to have the best of me, but I often feel like circumstances suffocate the "best me." With all the anger, bitterness, emptiness, and sadness swirling within me, how can I bless my family with my presence?

In countless ways, God's truth has helped me cope with the unpredictability and harshness of life in a fallen world. I'll briefly share two. First, the supremacy of God allows my emotions to be felt but doesn't give them the final say. It tames my feelings. When my emotions drag me inward, God's truth reminds me that there's more, a better story I am a part of. My suffering is not as lonely as it feels; it is a form of fellowshipping with Christ, sharing in his sufferings. When I feel like a spiritual outcast, I remember Christ and return to reality. I hold to what is true about God and, therefore, what is true of me even if all the emotional "evidence" contradicts it. Eventually my emotions snap back to the reality of God's goodness in the good news of Christ's life, death, resurrection, reign, and return.

Second, taking God's truth more seriously than my unruly emotions gives me opportunities to experience what J. R. R. Tolkien called a "eucatastrophe." Tolkien coined this term to describe when the unexpected occurs and it is good, "a sudden and miraculous grace," "a fleeting glimpse of Joy, Joy beyond the walls of the world, poignant as grief."[11] When we surrender to the guidance of the good Creator, then truth, beauty, and wonder pop out of the most unlikely of places. He grants us a glimpse of true joy, poignant as grief.

Precious little Jane is one of the most powerful eucatastrophes I have ever known. I weep for joy at the thought of her. She is not the gift Sheryl and I thought we were receiving; she is far better. She is joy incarnate. In light of who God is, I can truly see Jane for who she is. And I can truly see myself, all thanks to the powerful work of Jesus Christ. Apart from him, our emotions lead us away from wonder, away from beauty, away from the solid footholds that help you take the next step in a pain-ridden world. Trust him more than you trust your emotions.

—Trevor

You can show love for Trevor and the Wright family: https://www.gofundme.com/f/help-trevor-fight-stage-4-colon-cancer?qid=ff0496bd8ac3dcb8489a8c5cb9b0291d.

A Heretic's Prayer

God,
Shatter the primrose glasses of our self-serving bias so we
can see ourselves honestly. You are perfect. We are not. Help
us practice the discipline of meditating on your words so
frequently that your truth wins out over the lies we believe.
May your thoughts become our thoughts. Replace the
catastrophizing, generalizing, and blaming in our minds
with "whatever is true, whatever is honorable, whatever
is just, whatever is pure, whatever is lovely, whatever
is commendable" (Phil. 4:8). And by the Holy Spirit, the
omnipotent third person of the Trinity, would you kill the sarx,
the anti-God, antilife, self-destructive drives inside us. Replace
them with your love, joy, peace, patience, kindness, goodness,
faithfulness, gentleness, and self-control. Amen.

A Heretic's Field Manual

Before moving on to the next chapter, do three or four of the following to sharpen your skills at violating #theanswersare-within commandment:

1. Read Galatians 5:19–21 and pay attention to how Paul describes the works of the flesh. If Paul were writing to you instead of the first-century church in Galatia, what deeds of the sin nature might he include? Try to identify at least three. Take those immediately to the cross.
2. Read Galatians 5:22–23 about the fruit of the Spirit. The original Greek enlists something called a genitive of production to convey that this fruit is *produced by* the Spirit. Pray through the list, pausing at each one and identifying an area of your life where you most desperately need the Spirit to produce that particular fruit.
3. Take another look at Lukianoff and Haidt's list of nine cognitive distortions. Pinpoint your top two or three. Ask the Holy Spirit to go to work resetting your psyche and to replace your distortions with his reality.
4. For one week, carve out a few minutes each morning to read Ephesians 1. Throughout your day, meditate on what this passage affirms about who God is and who you are.
5. To get better at biblical CBT, form a habit of meditating on a psalm before you fall asleep.

#authentic

Thou shalt invent and advertise thine own identity.

We are so many things, all the time. And I know it can be overwhelming figuring out who to be. . . . I have some good news: It's totally up to you. I also have some terrifying news: It's totally up to you.
—Taylor Swift, singer

Christianity came into the world firstly in order to assert with violence that a man had not only to look inwards but to look outwards, to behold with astonishment and enthusiasm a divine company and a divine captain. The only fun of being a Christian was that a man was not left alone with the inner light, but definitely recognized an outer light fair as the sun.
—G. K. Chesterton, writer

Today, one of the worst things you can possibly be is inauthentic. There is a fascinating history behind the rise of authenticity as a chief virtue in the United States. The 1950s supplied a portrait of an all-American, hardworking, well-paid patriarch in a suit and tie. He returns from the office each day to his trim bride in a patterned dress, with a three-course supper on the table. His kids, Dick and Jane, rush to the door to wrap their arms around his neck. Their lawn is pristine, they pay their taxes, and they bring casserole to the neighborhood social. Structure, self-determination, community, convention—the modern man. Living by such old-fashioned social expectations is what many today mean by "inauthentic."

The Bourgeoisie versus the Bohemians

Over and against the modern man rises a generation of rebels championing authenticity against the soulless status quo.[1] One of the prophets of the rebellion was a beat poet named Allen Ginsberg. Bucking the materialism of modernity, Ginsberg famously had only one bowl in his barren apartment. In 1954 he published *Howl and Other Poems*, which became a kind of gospel for the 1960s counterculture—the anti-establishment, the despisers of phoniness and predictability, the new Romantics, the psychedelic space monkeys, the bohemians and hippies.

If *Howl* was the first of four gospels for the counterculture, then the second was Jack Kerouac's *On the Road* in 1957. Kerouac recounted his adventures with Dean Moriarty (the real-life Neal Cassady) as they traversed the country on the prowl for their next rush from jazz, crime, drugs, booze, or sex with strangers. Then came Herbert Marcuse's *One-Dimensional Man* (1964), a scathing critique of the soul-sucking side effects of modern consumerism. Next came Abbie Hoffman's *Steal This Book* (1971), a how-to guide for budding revolutionaries intent on overthrowing the "Pig Empire" that is "Amerika."

What tied these four gospels together (along with other staples of the counterculture canon like Huxley's *The Doors of Perception*, Kesey's *One Flew Over the Cuckoo's Nest*, and Vonnegut's *Slaughterhouse-Five*) was a shared sense of the hypocrisy, the plasticity, and the soullessness of mainstream modern culture. These authors and their readers embodied the spirit of authenticity long before the hashtag was invented. The Romantics of the eighteenth and nineteenth centuries did the same two centuries before the beatniks and hippies.

These counterculture artists got some things profoundly right. What they got right shines more vividly in the atmosphere of the Christian worldview than it does against the backdrop of the atheism, Marxism, or New Age mysticism that many embrace. God calls us to be fully human, and the modern mainstream can indeed be plastic and inhuman. We are image-bearers of God and, therefore, far more than profit-maximizers, the insignias on our cars, or cogs in a corporate machine. Rule-keeping for rule-keeping's sake is a path to losing your soul. Life's purpose must be more than climbing materialistic ladders. The natural world has more than instrumental value; it is not like toilet paper to be used on human rear ends, then flushed.

These are deeply Christian truths. They are true because God is there. He really created humanity in his image. He really saves us by grace. He really calls us to join him on a mission of redemption that transcends mere consumption, competition, and corporate ladder-climbing. These vital truths about being fully human collapse without sturdy biblical scaffolding to support them.

This collapse is exactly what happened when the hippies of the 1960s and 70s morphed into the yuppies of the 1980s. As the THC and psychedelics had diminishing returns, the counterculture's singing prophets dropped dead one by one (e.g., Hendrix, Joplin, Morrison each at the tender age of twenty-seven, as Cobain and Winehouse did a generation later), and as middle-age practicalities set in, the hippies turned into Wall Street types. Profit-seeking yuppies of the 80s inspired the jaded rage of the grunge movement in the 1990s. A generation of dot-com entrepreneurs sprouted up in the 2000s, followed by the hipster movement of the 2010s. We search for authenticity against the mainstream, that quest goes mainstream, the bohemians become bourgeoisie, and on it goes.

With each epoch shift, something rebelled against gets retained in the next rendition of rebellion. The hipster generation retained the technological infatuations and general consumer outlook of their yuppie predecessors. Today, big corporations fill their ads with Romantic appeals and saccharine Marxist utopian images and promises. This is all coalescing into the New Man of the twenty-first century—what David Brooks calls a "Bobo," a combination of the bourgeoisie and the bohemian—a self-obsessed bundle of contradictions, ever outraged yet apathetic, hungry as a tiger, fragile as an origami swan, empty as a vodka bottle, and bored as a caged parakeet.

This is where the pursuit of authenticity—devoid of God—has left us in our day. We're left with the predictable mantras of mainstream marketing telling us to be our most fabulous selves by bucking society's expectations.[2] The goal of life is to become "a 'self' liberated through experiences and strong feelings from the inhibiting constraints of social convention."[3] That's what many mean by "authentic."

For the Frederick Douglasses of history, authenticity was about courageously subverting forces that work against God's transcendent standards of truth, goodness, beauty, and justice. Today, being "authentic" means little more than tearing down any force that dares question,

> Today, being "authentic" means more than tearing down any force that dares question, challenge, or reject the self's sovereign expression of itself.

challenge, or reject the self's sovereign expression of itself. This new version of authenticity confronts us with three problems.

The Inconthievable Problem

One of the great lines in cinematic history comes from Inigo Montoya (Mandy Patinkin) in *The Princess Bride* (1987). When his Sicilian boss Vizzini (Wallace Shawn) repeats the word "inconthievable" (the heavily lisped version of "inconceivable"), Inigo remarks, "You keep using that word. I do not think it means what you think it means."[4]

The same could be said for the way our culture deploys the word "authentic." There's a better word to describe treating our own desires as unquestionable and stigmatizing everyone who does not celebrate our desires as an oppressor. The right word is "arrogant." Arrogance elevates our feelings on a golden candle-lit altar for everyone else to grovel and bow before. Authenticity says, "God made me an emotional being, but my emotions are not God. My feelings can be right or wrong. I'm not perfect. I often get angry at the wrong things, love some things too much and others too little, enjoy some of the wrong things and yawn at some of the most joyous things." Arrogance says, "All my feelings are right." Authenticity says, "I need the Heart Surgeon to repair this broken organ in my chest."

God is not emotionally fractured. His feelings (if they could even be called that) are eternally perfect and just. If the Creator enjoys something, then it is truly joyous. If God rages at something, we can trust that it is truly outrageous. If God laughs at something—such as nations plotting against him—then it is truly laughable.[5] When we erase the Creator-creature distinction, we ascribe emotional perfection to ourselves. We assume that granting our feelings sacred status is what it means to be "authentic." Creatures pretending they are the Creator is the essence of arrogance. Today's champions of authenticity can't survive Inigo Montoya's riposte: "I do not think it means what you think it means."

The Weight Problem

In a refreshingly honest article, Jane Caro said, "We are not fabulous. . . . No one is. We are all flawed, insecure, tired, self-indulgent, often bewildered human beings who mostly struggle to stay on top of the demands of everyday life."[6] Amen. In one sense, we are all far more fabulous than we realize—as eternal beings uniquely reflecting the divine image. In another sense, we are hardly as fabulous as we like to think we are.

The apostle Paul had a sterling religious résumé: "Circumcised on the eighth day, of the people of Israel, of the tribe of Benjamin, a Hebrew of Hebrews; as to the law, a Pharisee," and all the rest (Phil. 3:5–6). Rather than flaunting himself, he compares all his self-powered spiritual accomplishments to a steaming pile of dung (3:8). The Reformer Martin Luther was often the literal butt of his own jokes, and was rumored to say that when he farted in Wittenberg, they could smell it in Rome. G. K. Chesterton, weighing over three hundred pounds, frequently made light of his not-so-light self. When struggling to fit into a horse-drawn carriage, the story goes, the cabbie suggested he try entering sideways, to which Chesterton replied, "I no longer have a sideways."[7]

When we take God seriously, we discover one of life's most

glorious freedoms—the freedom to not take ourselves seriously. Having gravitas for God and levity about ourselves, we float peacefully above the sheer exhaustion of an ever offended culture. Looking to Jesus and laughing at ourselves go hand in hand. Per usual, Chesterton says it better than I can: "A characteristic of the great saints is their power of levity. Angels can fly because they can take themselves lightly. . . . Pride is the downward drag of all things into an easy solemnity. . . . Satan fell by the force of gravity."[8]

> **Looking to Jesus and laughing at ourselves go hand in hand.**

I can't imagine a more devastating weight than the command to be #authentic. Finite you, with your issues and imperfections, must construct an entire identity for yourself. Then, you must sustain that identity through all the jarring twists and turns of life. Then, you must successfully market that identity to others and hope they don't see the quivering self behind the slick, filtered image. How exhausting!

We were never meant to live that way. The task of constructing and sustaining an identity over time is literally a God-sized task. Forcing that responsibility onto our all-too-shaky and finite shoulders is just plain mean. People all around us are buckling under that impossible weight. The more bombarded we are with the dogma of defining ourselves, the more depression and anxiety records we break.[9]

Authenticity puts an especially unbearable weight on children. Literally, as I write these sentences in my courtyard, a car has pulled into my street, to my left, blasting the *Frozen* hit "Let It Go," Elsa's anthem to self-authorship. "No right, no wrong, no rules for me, I'm freeee!"[10] At the same moment, to my right, *My Little Pony: The Movie* is playing in my living room with the tune "Time to Be Awesome," with lyrics like "Be awesome, it's all up to you," and "take the Storm King's orders and toss 'em, cause it's the time to let our colors fly."[11] I am writing in the middle of an author-yourself sandwich, served up for little kids who don't realize the awesomeness they're being deprived of by trying to be their own sovereign authors. Time to put the laptop down and go talk to my girls about the Creator-creature distinction and the joy of living a life authored by God.

The Sun Problem

We move to a third and final problem with our twenty-first-century pursuit of our #authentic selves. This problem first struck me in, of all places, a Jean-Paul Sartre quote: "If you have a finite point and it has no infinite reference point, then that finite point is absurd."[12] I don't know if the French existentialist realized when he said it, but he made a knock-down, drag-out argument against authenticity.

Picture your psyche like a solar system. The particulars of your life make up the planets in your psychological solar system. There's a planet to represent your romantic status, one for your family life, your social life, your career, your finances, and so on. Here's the question: Where is the real *you* in that solar system? You would, no doubt, still be quintessentially yourself if any of those particulars changed. What fact about yourself makes for an authentic identity?

Put differently, which factor is stable and shiny enough to function like the Sun in your psyche, keeping all the other aspects of your identity in a meaningful orbit? Can you make your looks, your job, your romance, your religious performance, or anything else the center point of your identity? Is anything inside you big enough to be the ultimate integration point for everything else inside you?

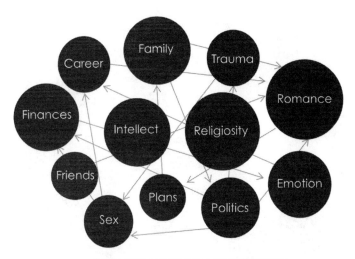

THE FINITE PARTICULARS OF YOUR IDENTITY

Because you are a creature and not the Creator, every particular of your life is finite and, thus, not big enough to bring order and purpose to every other part of you. Making some finite particular of your life the center point of who you are is a recipe for an identity crisis. Postmodern novelist David Foster Wallace made this point: "If you worship money and things . . . then you will never have enough. . . . Worship your body and beauty and sexual allure and you will always feel ugly. . . . Worship power, you will end up feeling weak and afraid."[13]

What we need is something more than a finite particular. We need an Infinite Universal at the center of our being to bestow meaning on all the particulars of who we are. We need what Jesus promises in John 14:17—the Holy Spirit, "who dwells with you and will be *in* you" (italics added). This is extraordinary. The Holy Spirit is not an impersonal force like electricity; he is the all-knowing, all-loving, all-powerful third person of the Holy Trinity. For those who trust Jesus, the Holy Spirit is not merely *with* us, but takes up permanent residence *in* us. As God, the Holy Spirit has all the mass and gravitas to hold us together.

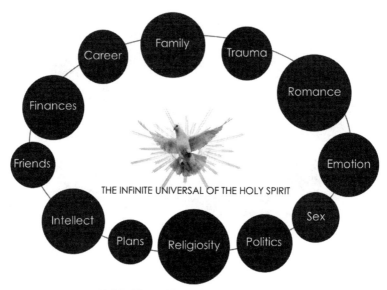

THE INFINITE UNIVERSAL OF THE HOLY SPIRIT

THE FINITE PARTICULARS OF YOUR IDENTITY

The Holy Spirit, in other words, has much to do with our very structure and design as human beings. A guitar, for example, was designed to be played. It brings powerful noise into the world in the hands of someone who knows what they're doing. A white Stratocaster didn't play "Little Wing" and "Voodoo Chile" by itself; it required a Hendrix. No parts of the guitar can play themselves. Left alone it will collect dust or tip over and make a dissonant clang. We were designed to add beauty to the world by being strummed by Someone beyond ourselves. That's where the Holy Spirit comes in. How can you fulfill your design and make good noise? It's as simple as asking the Holy Spirit to take a hold of you and strum away.

The Authored Life

What should we expect if we fully yield to the Holy Spirit this week? What happens when we allow our Creator to take us over?

Round-the-clock euphoria, a mountaintop high? No. Remember, God is not another acid trip. Rather, you can experience the deep meaning of an authored life. Let's briefly explore the meaning of the authored life in three passages.

In Ephesians 2, on the heels of affirming that we are saved by God's grace rather than our own spiritual performance, Paul says, "We are his workmanship, created in Christ Jesus for good works, which God prepared beforehand, that we should walk in them" (Eph. 2:10). Paul infused the whole passage with the language of an authored life.

The word for "workmanship" is *poiema* in the Greek, which some translations render "masterpiece." It is as if you are a hunk of jagged stone. God, the Master Sculptor, hammers and chisels away to make something jaw-droppingly spectacular out of you. Ephesians 2 echoes the Master-and-his-medium language of Isaiah 64:8: "We are the clay, and you are our potter; we are all the work of your hand." In the second part of Ephesians 2:10, Paul uses the word *ktisthentes*, meaning "having been created,"[14] followed by the teleological word "for" (ἐπὶ). God determines not only *that* we exist but also *why* we exist. Human nature, then, is not a bowl of alphabet soup—a senseless jumble of floating letters that can be arranged at our leisure. Human nature is like a book—we are authored beings with purpose we don't invent, but discover.

Paul says these masterpieces are designed to do good works that God *proetoimasen*, meaning "prepared beforehand." Far more meaning is scripted into your day than you realize. There are divine appointments, meaningful moments planned before you even stumble off the mattress. There have been countless days I thought I was just headed to the office, joining the neighbors for barbecue, catching a flight, or chatting around a fire pit. But God was up to something eternal and far more glorious than anything that could be caught on the dull video footage of the day. We only get occasional glimpses of the beautiful top of the tapestry; most of life is spent underneath the tapestry looking at a seemingly chaotic network of threads. Our pre-glory state-of-mind means we are usually missing the big picture. How many conversations in the new heaven and new earth will be about the glorious feats God pulled off through a forgotten conversation, shared coffee, or some other mundane encounter? There is real meaning in knowing that our days are filled with "good works prepared beforehand," especially in those inevitable seasons when life seems boring and hopeless.

Psalm 139 is a beautifully countercultural old hymn. Here the God-as-author motif is explicit: "In [God's] book were written, every one of them, the days that were formed for me, when as yet there were none of them" (v. 16). God being the author of his days is not a source of anxiety or feeling of oppression for the psalmist. It is radically liberating to live a life authored by Someone infinitely more creative and kind than we are.

The psalmist says we are "wonderfully made" (v. 14). This is the polar opposite of today's gospel in which we create our identities from scratch. Being wonderfully made frees us from the exhausting task of trying to conjure up and prove our own wonderfulness. "You hem me in, behind and before," the psalmist celebrates (v. 5). Rather than the vertigo and nausea of standing before an infinite expanse of options, the psalmist exults in the hemmed-in life. So should we. "Search me, O God, and know my heart! . . . See if there be any grievous way in me, and lead me in the way everlasting!" (vv. 23–24). Oh, the sweet freedom of not having to pretend we are perfect!

Embrace the lightheartedness and abundant purpose of the Other-authored life.

Lastly, we see the words of Jesus: "Whoever seeks to preserve his life will lose it, but whoever loses his life will keep it" (Luke 17:33). Let go of your need to define yourself. Don't get chewed up and spit out by an ideology of self-authorship.

Be countercultural. Lose yourself in Christ. Embrace the light-heartedness and abundant purpose of the Other-authored life. Live in sync with the Creator-creature distinction. Live the reality that God is God and you are not. That is true authenticity.

A Heretic's Testimonial

David Yohan Chung is from South Korea, a graduate of Biola University, an operatic voice performer, and a theologian-in-training. He is also a heretic to the cult of self-worship. He boldly breaks the #authentic commandment. This is his story.

I was born in Seoul, South Korea, twelve weeks prematurely. Although amazing medical technology helped saved my life, it had one nasty side effect. I received too much oxygen in my brain and ended up with a visual impairment. The Korean culture I was born into was saturated with superstition, including the vicious lie that contact with someone who has a disability brings bad luck. My childhood was marked by people hurling curses and spitting on me. So my parents brought me to the United States. Here I faced a new form of discrimination when one of my teachers found out I was an immigrant. I snapped. I was mad at God and harbored thoughts of hopelessness and suicide in my heart. I was raised in the church but, up until this point, had no personal relationship with my Creator. I concluded that my life had no purpose.

Thankfully, I was wrong. Jesus met me in my deepest, darkest night of despair. What I had learned about him at church turned out to be far more real than I had imagined. Bombarded by God's grace and lovingkindness, I fell on my knees and accepted the everlasting gift of life that only Jesus Christ can give. As an ethnic minority with a disability, I could have taken another life path, that of a victim, feeling perpetually sorry for myself. Instead, I chose life as a victor in Christ Jesus. He is my wholeness. He is my perfection. He defines me.

Korean culture sends a strong message that you must never, under any circumstances, shame your family. That usually means attending an Ivy League school and becoming either a lawyer, engineer, doctor, businessman, or accountant. And that's what my heart was telling me to do as well. Then, God threw a curveball my way that I did not see coming (no pun intended). God made it clear that he wanted me to enroll not at Harvard or Stanford but at a Christian university called Biola. I was to audition for Biola University's Conservatory of Music with a focus on operatic voice performance, a step even further beyond my plan.

Letting God author my life rather than trying to author my own life was the turning point. God took care of me in the most outrageous ways possible. I graduated in 2019, after God provided over $175,000 in scholarships, grants, and countless financial gifts from friends who love Jesus. My story is still unfolding, but I am sure of this—God's sovereign ability to author our lives is far more interesting, meaningful, surprising, and joyful than anything we could dream up for ourselves. It's not always easy, but then again God never promised us the easy road. But it is meaningful. I have the awesome privilege of experiencing God's loving-kindness on a daily basis. You can too. Simply ask for it.

—David

A Heretic's Prayer

God,
You are God and we are not. You are infinitely better at
being God than we are, but we fool ourselves daily. We take
ourselves too seriously. God, help us to take you so seriously
that we can laugh at ourselves. We try to self-author, when
the days you have written for us are far more meaningful.
Help us to step into the good works you prepared beforehand
for us today and tomorrow. We try to be the sun in our own
psychological solar systems and end up spinning in chaos.
Holy Spirit, take your proper place at the center of our souls
and move the rest of us into proper orbit around you. Help us
to live authentically before the truth that you are the Creator
and we are creatures. Amen.

A Heretic's Field Manual

Before moving on to the next chapter, do three or four of the following to sharpen your skills at violating the commandment to be #authentic:

1. Think of five ways that God is far better at being God than we are. Pray through the list, thanking God for being God.

2. Think through the finite particulars that make up your identity. Identify the top three things, other than God, that you are most prone to make the center of your identity. In prayer, yield those things to God, one by one, asking him to take their place.

3. When you wake up, pray a simple prayer. "God, you have good works prepared beforehand for me to do today. Help me do them for your glory."

4. Use some self-deprecating humor, putting yourself in an unflattering light to others.

5. Take five minutes, no screens or distractions, and try to recall as many moments as you can where it was clear that God was up to something bigger and better than what you expected.

#livethedream

Thou shalt force the universe to bend to your desires.

We are here to fully introduce ourselves, to impose ourselves and ideas and thoughts and dreams onto the world. . . . So we cannot contort ourselves to fit into the visible order. We must unleash ourselves and watch the world reorder itself in front of our eyes.

—GLENNON DOYLE, SELF-HELP AUTHOR

For the wise men of old the cardinal problem had been how to conform the soul to reality, and the solution had been knowledge, self-discipline, and virtue. For magic and applied science alike the problem is how to subdue reality to the wishes of men.

—C. S. LEWIS, DIVINE-HELP AUTHOR

One of the most popular Disney credos is "If you can dream it, you can do it."[1] Cinderella captured the sentiment when she sang, "If you keep on believing, the dream that you wish will come true."[2] In a Tony Award–winning play called *Urinetown*—not exactly a Disney production—we find a very Disneyesque dialogue:

> **Bobby:** Follow my heart? But to where?
> **Hope:** To wherever your heart tells you to go.
> **Bobby:** Even . . . there?
> **Hope:** Even to the clouds, if that's what your heart
> commands.

Note the word "commands." It's not about what the Creator commands. It's not about us commanding our own hearts. Like dogs on a chain, it is about our hearts commanding us and our obedience.

On February 22, 2020, near Barstow, California, a daredevil flat-earth advocate named "Mad" Mike Hughes strapped into his homemade steam-powered rocket and followed his heart's command to the clouds. At takeoff, the landing parachutes deployed, throwing the rocket off its trajectory into a nosedive in the California desert. Tragically, Mike Hughes, image-bearer of God, did not survive the impact.

Reality has a structure. When we shun that structure and break reality's rules, reality has a way of breaking us back.[3] I don't mean only the structure and rules of physical reality but also the structure and rules of morality. Leap over the rail at the San

Clemente pier and it makes no difference whether you believe in the laws of gravity—the cold Pacific salt water is coming (and hopefully no great whites). Similarly, moral laws don't require your belief in them for them to do what they do.

Reality Breaks Back

Everything I just said is full-blown heresy against the doctrines of self-worship, which declare that the universe must bend around our dreams and desires. If I am a heretic, then I expect to see some of Hollywood's greatest writers and directors next to me at the flaming stake.

In Francis Ford Coppola's cinematic masterpieces *The Godfather* and *The Godfather Part II* (for true fans, there is no *Godfather Part III*), we witness the transformation of Michael Corleone (Al Pacino). He goes from a war hero carving out an identity away from "the family business," to the powerful new don of the Corleone organized-crime family. Along the way—spoiler alert—he murders a corrupt police captain and an aspiring drug lord in an Italian eatery. During his godson's baptism, Michael masterminds simultaneous hits on the heads of the other crime families. He sabotages his marriage and disowns his wife. *Part II* ends with an utterly solitary Michael sitting outside his beach house staring out on Lake Tahoe where he just had his brother Fredo murdered. Michael broke the structure of moral reality; reality broke him back.

That is a running theme of some of Hollywood's best films. In Brian De Palma's 1983 cult classic *Scarface*, we follow Tony Montaña (also Al Pacino) on his bloody rise from Cuban immigrant to Miami cocaine kingpin. To live his dream life, he brashly breaks God's commandments and becomes wildly prosperous by the world's standards.[4] In the closing sequence—spoiler alert—shortly after brandishing an M203 grenade launcher with the iconic line

"Say hello to my little friend!" Montaña takes an assassin's bullet to the back. He plummets off his balcony into the fountain in his gaudy mansion foyer. The water turns maroon as his corpse floats under his neon globe that ironically reads "The World Is Yours."

Here, art mirrors life. Several notable self-worshipers followed their hearts into booze and drug addictions, suicidal depression, STDs, devastated families, prisons, asylums, and early deaths. Life also mirrors art. My friend "Bruce" was a huge Pacino fan. A *Godfather* and a two-tone Tony Montaña poster hung proudly on his bedroom wall. It was obvious to anyone who had seen the films that Bruce patterned his personality, his turns of phrase, even his dreams and aspirations after these fictional gangsters. He once confided to me that he'd rather be feared than loved, a Machiavellian theme of both movies. He ran his nickel-and-dime Orange County pot-dealing operation out of his dingy apartment as if he were Michael Corleone expanding the family business or Tony Montaña closing a million-dollar coke deal from his Miami mansion. Reality broke Bruce back. Snubbing moral reality led to severed relationships, a police record, and a gaping, angry, easily offended hole in the center of his heart.

The good news is that because God exists, we are never broken beyond repair. I had the awesome privilege of a front row seat to Bruce's redemption. I sat two feet away on my scrappy red garage couch as he invited Jesus to heal his past pain of growing up with

Because God exists, we are never broken beyond repair.

a convict father and the relentless mockery of his schoolmates. I did his premarital counseling and stood three feet away as he exchanged rings and vows with his bride. I saw him win awards for his profound role as a mentor, turning around the lives of troubled young men. Bruce went from following his gangster dreams of power and prosperity to living in sync with the moral framework of reality as God structured it according to his holy nature. It has been a big move up for Bruce, and a real joy for me to behold.

Most of us probably don't aspire to be mob bosses or drug lords, but, like Bruce, we do feel the weight of constructing a compelling identity for the world. The possibilities seem limitless, especially as the structure of reality is increasingly shunned in the name of freedom. Heavily trafficked Gen Z platforms like TikTok offer a steady stream of influencers who school the next generation with insights like "There are transmen who lactate." One influencer who identifies as "a threat, a nightmare, and a goddess (so please bow down to me)" recommends Satanism, "which means I am my own god and I worship myself." Another influencer expressed her true self by marrying a roller coaster. There is a whole subculture of "furries"—people who dress and act like animals. About half of the furry community would like to be 0 percent human if they could.[5] The goal of life under this constant bombardment is not to live within reality but to force reality to bend around our subjective whims.[6]

If you attempt such boundless self-expression, then three problems confront you—the Pinocchio problem, the Little Mermaid problem, and the Elsa problem. That's a hat tip to Disney, the planet's biggest promoter of #livethedream propaganda.

The Pinocchio Problem

I was raised watching an Italian puppet strive to become a real boy. When Pinocchio ignores his conscience—the voice of moral reason personified as a crooning cricket in a top hat—he abandons his family for the fame and fortune of Stromboli's stage. The result is lonesome imprisonment. When he breaks the moral order again by lying, Pinocchio sprouts an ugly tree branch for a nose. When he transgresses against moral reality for the reckless fun of Pleasure

Island, Pinocchio becomes even less human, sprouting a tail and furry ears and braying like a donkey.

When the wooden boy syncs his actions with the moral realities of love and courage, sacrificing his life to save his family from the vicious sea monster, Monstro, he is "resurrected" as a real boy. The message, even to my five-year-old self, was clear. Doing whatever you want is not the way to real-boy-ness. It's the way to make an ass out of yourself. We must live out realities like love and courage to really live. There are real goods that lead to more authentic humanness and real evils that lead to dehumanization. It is a tale that makes sense only if there is a moral structure to reality.

Contrast the thick, layered moral world of *Pinocchio* with the paper-thin and flat world of a more recent Disney production, *Small Potatoes*. This animated Disney Jr. show features tunes like "I Just Want to be Me,"[7] a potato-sung punk anthem about self-expression and not letting anyone tell you who to be. The episode "We're All Potatoes at Heart" concludes with a potato telling an audience of impressionable minds, "I think it's great to be different and unique because then everyone has their own different way of doing things, and there's no wrong or right answer for doing something."[8]

Thousands of years ago a devious serpent promised that humans could define the reality of good and evil for themselves. Over a hundred years before talking potatoes, Nietzsche wrote *Beyond Good and Evil* to convince his readers to become supermen who ignore all external standards, especially Christianity's "right and wrong answer for doing something." In the 1960s, Sartre argued that "if God does not exist . . . everything is

The cruelty of our age is peddling the lie to kids that they can create their own moral universes.

permissible."[9] It is no longer the serpent, a mustachioed German, or a walleyed French existentialist, it is an adorable animated potato redefining freedom as doing whatever we want.

The cruelty of our age is peddling the lie to kids that they can create their own moral universes. Lord, have mercy on the Disney scriptwriters; they know not what they do (or do they?)—misleading kids with a serpentine message of self-definition that yields nothing but arrogance, anxiety, depression, and hell.[10]

The Little Mermaid Problem

Not only does #livethedream defile kids with an ancient lie that makes true heroism impossible, it also makes us unnecessarily anxious as we chart our courses into the future. The future, like a two-year-old or teenage human, tends to not heed our orders. The future's unknowns really rain on our self-glorifying parades. Who knows if some dream-crushing news is just around the corner? We can try our best to mastermind future outcomes to realize our dreams, but so much is beyond our control. The universe is stubborn and inscrutable, and we are not all-knowing. Attempt to crack the code of the future and your frustration, resentment, and anxiety will overtake you.

As we look toward the future, one thing is certain. A miniscule percentage of those chasing the dream actually #livethedream, at least the way "the dream" is typically (and shallowly) understood. Here is an exchange between early YouTube sensation turned highly lucrative comic Bo Burnham and Conan O'Brien on *Conan*:

> **Conan:** You must have a lot of young people that say, Bo, how do I accomplish what you've accomplished. What's your advice for young people?
> **Bo:** Well, you gotta just take a deep breath and [pregnant pause] give up . . . [laughter]. Don't take advice from people like me who've gotten very lucky. Taylor Swift telling you to follow your dreams is like a lottery

winner saying liquidize your assets, buy Powerball tickets, it works. It doesn't, you won't.[11]

According to the National Collegiate Athletic Association (NCAA), about a half million out of eight million teens playing high school sports will make it to college sports. One in sixteen isn't too terrible. But from there the numbers of those who #livethedream plummet dramatically. In 2019 less than 10 percent of the 8,002 NCAA baseball players were drafted into the major leagues. The NBA drafted a measly 1.2 percent of NCAA draft-eligible players. It was .08 percent for the WNBA. Out of 16,380 draft-eligible football players, only 254 ended up in the NFL, just 1.5 percent.[12]

The proportions of those who fail in the music and movie industries are even more dismal. And who can count how many seek social media stardom and end up with fifty views, most of which are clicks from themselves and their mom? The call to #livethedream ignores how much of a crapshoot life is and how few people make it to the so-called top. Moreover, when you peer into the lives of many at the top—the .0000000001 percent—the dream they are living often seems more like a waking nightmare. Thankfully, there is a better way.

My daughters love the Little Mermaid ride—Ariel's Undersea Adventure—at the Disney California Adventure Park. They could ride those giant seashells under the sea *ad infinitum ad nauseum*. (One ride took a dark turn in 2018. Our shell stalled out in Ursula's cave, and my girls started screaming when the sea witch's animatronic head flopped off, revealing a tangle of rainbow wiring and circuits, as her evil anthem "Poor Unfortunate Souls" looped on the sound system. The incident made the Orange County papers.[13]) A year or so before that horrifying moment, I entered the park with my toddler riding my shoulders. Harlow, four at the time, had enough spatial awareness to know that from the park entrance Ariel's

Undersea Adventure is straight ahead, then a slight veer to the right. Instead, I hung a sharp right that seemed to take us way off course.

She didn't throw a tantrum. She didn't panic. She was happily perched on my shoulders without a care in the world. Why? Simple. She trusts her daddy. She knows not only that I love her, that her joy matters to me, but also that I am smarter than her, although she's gaining on me by the day.

To a four-year-old intellect, that sharp right turn made no sense whatsoever. But it didn't have to. She knew that an older, wiser mind directed her course. So she had peace. No need to worry. And, indeed, as I could see the huge traffic jam of bodies forming on Buena Vista Street for the imminent Pixar parade, there was a perfectly good reason for our sharp right turn. A shortcut past the Redwood Creek Challenge would save time. What would seem illogical, and perhaps even cruel to a less trusting, more hubristic preschooler, was, in reality, a logical step. Because she trusted me, my daughter was able to truly enjoy an amusement park as an *amuse*ment park. To muse is to think, and the prefix *a-* means "not," so amusement is the ability to have fun without having to think and analyze everything.

When we move from California Adventure to the cosmos, the lesson is clear. If we believe there is no being with a higher IQ running the show—no good Father with a capital *F* guiding our life course—then we no longer experience the cosmos for the amusement park it is often meant to be. We become overanalytical and anxious. We become like a morbid astrophysicist descending into the darkness of Disneyland's Space Mountain as the stars flash by, refusing to enjoy himself until

When we try to #livethedream by making ourselves the standards of reality, we miss out on much of life.

he can calculate everything around him, rather than simply enjoying the unquantifiable rush of twisting and twirling on an unpredictable trek through space. When we try to #livethedream by making ourselves the standards of reality, we miss out on much of life by being preoccupied and anxious. When we trust God as our good Father, we can enjoy the ride.

The Elsa Problem

My oldest daughter, Gracelyn, was eight at the time and wanted a lesson on drawing the most profitable icon of the modern age, Mickey Mouse. With sharpened number two pencils and fresh paper, we began. I explained how to angle our pencils and apply only light pressure to sketch the basic shape of that oval head with two big ear circles on top. Then came a horizontal oval and two vertical ovals for the nose and eyes, an arch for the bridge of the nose, and an elongated banana for the trademark smile. My drawing was slowly approximating the image of the world's most famous mouse. I turned to my daughter's sketch, which was, well, the stuff of nightmares. She had done the opposite of everything I had tried to teach her. The result was a razor-toothed demon spawn in unerasable thick black graphite.

When I asked her what went wrong, her reply was, "You have your way to draw Mickey, and I have mine. Neither is right or wrong, they're just different." I was being schooled in the dogmas of expressive individualism by an eight-year-old.

"It sort of sounds like you're quoting Elsa from *Frozen* when she sang, 'No right, no wrong, no rules for me, I'm free!'" I said. She nodded affirmatively.

"Well, let's think this through together." Aware of the deeply Christian roots of the story from Hans Christian Andersen's 1844 fairy tale "Snedronningen," or "The Snow Queen," I asked, "What do you think happened to Elsa's kingdom when she bucked all the rules to do her own thing? Was that good or bad for her kingdom?"

"Bad," she answered. Indeed, with no summer sun to grow the crops, Arendelle nearly starves and freezes to death.

"So it seems everybody just doing their own thing doesn't always go well. Maybe there actually are right and wrong ways to do things." Her next Mickey portrait was slightly less terrifying.

Without using the word, Gracey and I'd just had a conversation about teleology. "Teleology" is a fifty-cent word for what something or someone is made for—its purpose or design. A lawn mower has a *telos* to mow lawns. A toaster has a *telos* to toast bread. The extent to which they do what they were made to do is the extent to which they are, we may say, *fulfilled* mowers and toasters. If you ignore that *telos* and tip a lawnmower on its side in your living room and get that blade whirring as a makeshift fan on a hot day, it will not end well. If, on a cold day, you put your chilly hands in the toaster and pull down the lever, you will regret it.

The starry cosmos, with all its supernovas, glowing space dust, and shimmering gasses, has a *telos*. It is to "declare the glory of God" (Ps. 19:1). The nation of Israel was created and chosen with a *telos* for his glory (Isa. 49:1–3). They were rescued from Egyptian bondage, granted a king, a temple, victory over the Canaanites, protection from their Assyrian attackers, and restoration from Babylonian captivity all "for his name's sake."

What propelled Jesus to the fatal agonies of the cross and the infusion of indestructible life into his cold corpse? What drove the Holy Spirit to inspire Scripture and comfort, counsel, convict, enlighten, empower, and indwell saints? Why did God predestine outcasts to be his heaven-bound sons and daughters? Why will Jesus return to usher his saints into never-ending joy and the non-saints into never-ending damnation? The answer remains the same across the story of Scripture. It is the same answer to the question, "What is our *telos*?" We exist to "ascribe to the LORD the glory due his name" (Ps. 96:8), "to the praise of is glory" (Eph. 1:12, 14), "so that the name of our Lord Jesus may be glorified" (2 Thess. 1:12), that your life and mine would shout together Paul's anthem, "to him be glory forever" (Rom. 11:36). The glory of the triune God is a recurring melody from Genesis to Revelation.[14]

We ignore our *telos* to our own destruction. We violate our deepest being when we say, "No, my purpose is to gratify my sexual urges," or "I define the meaning of my own biology." There is a theocentric (God-centered) shape to the universe. Within that structure, we are born teleological beings made *by* him and *for* him. Glorifying and enjoying him is how we become fulfilled human beings. Glorifying ourselves is how we make asses of ourselves. Life is not a matter of believing our self-centered dreams intensely enough that reality bends around our wishes. The human who self-identifies as a bunny would not sprout long furry ears or poop bunny pellets. The self-identifying wolf wouldn't last long in the wolf pack. The self-identifying eagle wouldn't survive the leap off the skyscraper. Encouraging aspiring bunnies, wolves, and eagles to live their dreams does not make us loving, it makes us complicit in their destruction.

The Great Commission to "make disciples" includes offering others something far more hopeful than the self-destructive attempt to impose their dreams on the world. It is calling people to drop out of the mass-marketed revolt against reality and step into the godward flow of creation. It is the invitation to know, obey, love, and enjoy the God who made, rules, and redeems the world in Christ. Living out our true God-given *telos*, rather than trying to dream up our own meaning, is how we become the least alienated, most connected version of ourselves. Break the structure of reality and it will break you back. Step into the current of creation to glorify the

> **Encouraging aspiring bunnies, wolves, and eagles to live their dreams does not make us loving, it makes us complicit in their destruction.**

Creator and you will find a depth and richness of meaning beyond imagination.

A Heretic's Testimonial

Alisa Childers is a former rock star turned bestselling author, speaker, apologist, and podcaster (alisachilders.com). She is also a heretic against the cult of self-worship. She boldly breaks the #livethedream commandment. This is her story.

I'd like to tell you about the day I gave up on my big dream. *It was the smartest thing I've ever done.* As early as eleven years old, I knew exactly what I would be when I grew up. After a brief stint of believing I was going to be an Olympic gymnast, I knew I would be a Christian recording artist who would lead people to Jesus with her music.

But nothing happened.

I wrote dozens of songs, practiced guitar and piano, recorded demos in the home studio in my dad's bonus room, and even played little concerts here and there whenever churches would let me. I started getting older, and by twenty-five (that's practically a senior citizen in the music biz) the big dream still hadn't materialized. But then an opportunity came along to be a part of the contemporary Christian music group ZOEgirl. What a ride. We played music all over the world to hundreds of thousands of people, and I'm grateful for every second I got to spend doing it. For many people, this would be the very definition of living the dream.

But it wasn't my dream.

My dream never happened. Although I'm so glad the Lord gave me the opportunity to minister to many young girls who listened to ZOEgirl, I still had an unfulfilled longing. If I would have picked up the latest self-help book or listened to prevailing cultural wisdom, I should have continued to pound the pavement and smash down any door that stood between me and my successful solo music career. But there I was, in my midthirties, and I finally surrendered my dream to God. Had I really never done that? Had I been chasing some big "calling" for my life that God never intended me to have?

Friends, I literally gave up on my dreams. And guess what? God had a way better plan for me. After a crushing faith crisis, he led me to study apologetics and rebuilt the faith that had been torn down by the clever arguments I'd encountered in a progressive church. This led to the ministry I have now. Although it reaches far fewer people than my "dream ministry," it is more satisfying and thrilling than any dream I could ever cook up on my own.

And here's the kicker.

Even this ministry that God has blessed me with is not who I am but simply what I do in this moment. It may not be what I do forever. My assignment is the same as any other Christian, which is to "make disciples of all nations" (Matt. 28:19). Jesus said, "The last will be first" (Matt. 20:16), and, "Greater love has no man than he lay down his life for his friends" (John 15:13 RSV). Jesus never said to follow our hearts, chase our dreams, and find ourselves. He said we must *deny* ourselves, pick up our crosses, and follow him. This is where true freedom, hope, and deep joy abide.

—Alisa

A Heretic's Prayer

God,

You created us to be creative like you. One of the first commands you ever gave humanity was to bear your image by multiplying the net beauty in the universe. You granted us that extraordinary creative freedom to be expressed within the forms of creation you established. And you didn't structure reality to be a prude or a killjoy but for our flourishing and true freedom. Lord, forgive us for falling for the temptation to dream up our own realities in revolt against your sovereignty. When we break the moral reality you established, it breaks us back. Please forgive us and put us back together. Help us to obey and enjoy you, to trust you as our good Father, to glorify you as the supreme source of all that is good, true, and beautiful. May we lay our dreams at your feet and submit our desires to your will, that we may work for your glory and the good of others. Amen.

A Heretic's Field Manual

Before moving on to the next chapter, do three or four of the following to sharpen your skills at violating the commandment to #livethedream:

1. Read the real Ten Commandments recorded in Exodus 20 (not to be confused with the ten commandments of self-worship). Pray for the Holy Spirit's help to obey the commandments throughout your day.

2. Think of three ways you have broken the structure of moral reality. Think of how reality has broken you back. Ask Jesus to redeem those broken parts.

3. Think of three people who are currently being broken for their rebellion against moral reality. Pray for them by name, that God would redeem them.

4. Sometimes phrases like "glorifying God" can sound abstract and otherworldly. Spend fifteen minutes reading through one of the four Gospels to behold how Jesus—the greatest God-glorifier ever—incarnates what it means to live a God-centered life. When you're done, ask the Holy Spirit to form those theocentric habits in you this week.

5. What are three things you can't control that have been causing stress, frustration, and anxiety? Prayerfully yield them to the Father.

#loveislove

Thou shalt celebrate all lifestyles and love-lives as equally valid.

Modern man quite properly considers the conception of love to be overwhelmingly important as he looks at personality. Nevertheless, he faces a very real problem as to the meaning of love. Though modern man tries to hang everything on the word love, love can easily degenerate into something very much less because he really does not understand it. He has no adequate universal for love.
—FRANCIS SCHAEFFER, CHRISTIAN APOLOGIST

I might feel more attraction toward a reductionistic approach to sex if . . . I sensed that the sexual revolution had increased respect between genders, created a more loving environment for children, relieved the ache of personal loneliness, and fostered intimacy. I have seen no such evidence.
—PHILIP YANCEY, AUTHOR / BOB ROSS DOPPELGÄNGER

We have seen that self-worship promises us our best lives, cutting-edge lifestyles, liberated hearts, originality, tolerance, adventure, inner enlightenment, authenticity, and fulfilled dreams. When we poke through the paper-thin propaganda of ad men, social media influencers, professors, and dancing potatoes, we find the truth. Self-worship robs us of awe, makes us hypertraditionalists, shackles us to our hearts, makes us unwitting devotees to several creeps, steals our courage, makes life intolerably dull, and makes us befuddled, arrogant, and broken. In this final chapter we expose a final line of bogus advertising. Self-worship tells us that #loveislove. In reality, it makes haters and bigots of us all.

Word Makers and Civilization Breakers

The word "love" has been redefined in our self-worshipping age. Words matter. They hold the power to illuminate or obfuscate truth and, therefore, the power to make or break civilizations. The great minds behind dystopian literature understood this well.[1]

In Ray Bradbury's *Fahrenheit 451* the "firemen" of America's future "were given a new job," namely burning books, "as custodians of our peace of mind . . . official censors, judges, and executors."[2] In our day, such fiction is becoming nonfiction. The self-appointed "custodians of our peace of mind" at Brandeis University's Prevention, Advocacy, & Resource Center (PARC) inform us that the phrases "killing two birds with one stone," and "beating a dead horse" "normalize violence against animals." "Prostitute" should become "person who engages in sex work." "Facebook stalking" should become "researching online." Even the term "trigger warning" should be replaced with "content note" because "trigger warning" can be, well, too triggering. PARC's "Suggested Language List" was recently known as "The Oppressive Language List."[3] Ironically, this bothered some people, and they had to change the old title because it "centered . . . words and phrases that may cause harm."[4]

Winston Smith, the protagonist of George Orwell's *1984*, spent his days changing words so that "Newspeak" could twist reality to fit the Party's totalitarian agenda. Atop the concrete pyramid of Oceania's propaganda department—ironically titled the "Ministry of Truth"—hung the Party slogan in which "war," "slavery," and "ignorance" were redefined as "peace," "freedom," and "strength."

In C. S. Lewis's *That Hideous Strength*—my personal favorite dystopian story—we meet Mark Studdock. Like Orwell's Smith, Studdock is tasked with "concocting the news"[5] to drum up support for a tyrannical regime, the National Institute of Coordinated Experiments (N.I.C.E.). The goose-stepping police force of N.I.C.E. is euphemized as "sanitary executives."[6] N.I.C.E. itself is a euphemism for what, in reality, is a cadre of pseudoscientific nihilists in league with satanic principalities (renamed "Macrobes"), to put "man on the throne of the universe," which really amounts to "the abolition of man."[7]

Euphemisms abound today.[8] It is not the termination of a genetically unique preborn human being (not only a theological but also a scientific fact)—it is "the evacuation of uterine contents" or removing "a clump of cells," like "unpersons" in *1984*'s Newspeak. Any opposition to the procedure is renamed a "war on women," regardless of the real harm the greedy abortion industry does to both fully grown and tiny women.[9]

If you question whether such words actually help people or correspond to reality, a slew of damning labels has been invented to scare and ultimately silence you. "In the end," wrote Orwell, "the

Party would announce that two and two made five, and you would have to believe it."[10] By the logic of certain elites in our world, the only conceivable reason that you do not parrot their ever evolving lingo is if you are a bigot, hater, or phobic. You must, therefore, be either reeducated or silenced. (Usually, the best way to spot real bigots, haters, or phobics is to find those running around calling everyone else bigots, haters, or phobics.)

Resisting these word games has nothing to do with hating or fearing people. We resist because ideologues have weaponized several important words to deny external reality and demand our unquestioning cowlike obedience. Given the power of words to reveal or revolt against reality, Christianity has a long history of taking words seriously. As Jesus himself said, "By your words you will be justified, and by your words you will be condemned" (Matt. 12:37). We must hold fast to that noble tradition. Be a heretic against the cult of self-worship

> Given the power of words to reveal or revolt against reality, Christianity has a long history of taking words seriously.

by making a daily habit of calling things by their true names.

More than "Two Minutes and Fifty-Two Seconds"

How, then, has the meaning of the word "love" changed in our day? Johnny Rotten of the Sex Pistols famously said, "Love is just two minutes and fifty-two seconds of squishing noises." If there is no God and a purely naturalistic story of human origins is true, then it is difficult to see why Rotten is wrong to reduce love to a brute sex act. If we are the lucky byproducts of millions of random mutations plus natural selection, then we have little place for love as anything more than swapping bodily fluids for survival's sake.[11] Whatever "love" means, it certainly means more than that.

For a more profound meaning of love, let's start in my garage.

Between two overcrowded bookshelves and above a beat-up piano hangs a gigantic piece of spray-painted stencil art entitled "Love Is Not a Sentimental Buzzword." The title sits below the stenciled heads of fifteen great minds, each with a quote helping define love.

Ponder their quotes and see what they add to your understanding and enjoyment of love:

The LORD your God will circumcise your hearts so that you will **love** him and live.

—MOSES

Two are better than one, so enjoy life with your wife whom you **love**.

—SOLOMON

May the **love** with which you **loved** me be in them, for you **loved** me, Father, before the world's foundation.

—JESUS

May God cause you to increase and abound in **love**.

—PAUL

Dear brothers, let us **love** one another because love comes from God.

—JOHN

Love God and do whatever you will.

—AUGUSTINE

Love is not a lifeless image but the living essence of the divine nature which beams full of all goodness.

—MARTIN LUTHER

Virtue is **love** to God, Being of beings, infinitely greatest and best.

—Jonathan Edwards

It is the great end of religion to make us **love** as good husbands, good fathers, and friends.

—William Wilberforce

Love man, even in his sin, for that is a likeness of divine **love**.

—Fyodor Dostoevsky

We will be a Christ-**loving** people or cease to be a people.

—Aleksandr Solzhenitsyn

Love's origin is not in chance but in that which has always been.

—Francis Schaeffer

Without **love** I'm barely human.

—Johnny Cash

Here we have love as something far more than an evolutionary aphrodisiac. Love is not a product of a million and a half random mutations. It existed before there were any molecules or cells to mutate. "Love comes from God" (John). As the self-giving community of the Father, the Son, and the Holy Spirit, love is indeed "the living essence of the divine nature" (Luther). In John 17:24 Jesus says, "Father . . . you loved me before the foundation of the world." Love really does have its origin "in that which has always been" (Schaeffer). Love predates the big bang, the Milky Way, the earth, the human race, hate, racism, and loneliness.[12]

The first time God looked into his creation and said something "is not good" is when he saw that man, Adam, was all alone (Gen.

2:18). So he created Eve, and now that interpersonal human love was possible, God declared his creation not only good but "very good" (Gen. 1:31). Relationship, connection, and intimacy are at the core of who we were made to be. Without them "we cease to be a people" (Solzhenitsyn) and are "barely human" (Cash).

Here we find still another case of the science slowly catching up to the Scriptures. Harvard researcher Robert Putnam found that "if you belong to no groups but decide to join one, you cut your risk of dying the next year *in half*."[13] Another study found that relationally well-connected people with bad health habits—smoking, poor diet, and/or heavy drinking—outlive isolated people with healthy habits. Relationally disconnected people were *three times* more likely to die than connected people![14]

The moral of the story is not to go chug a bottle of gin, chain-smoke a carton of cigarettes, and cram a greased-up pepperoni pizza down your gullet. The moral is that two really are "better than one" (Solomon). We were created by a God *of* community *for* community. We thrive when we are connected. First, we must connect with God, "Being of beings, infinitely greatest and best" (Edwards). Second, we must connect with one another as "good husbands, good fathers, and friends" (Wilberforce). (We might add, good wives, mothers, and neighbors.)

These authors aren't offering us cheap sentimental slogans printed on wooden rectangles in the home décor section of Target. They recognize that love, as central as it is

> **Loving God reorders our will and affections toward the good of others.**

to our nature, does not come naturally. Self-worship is our fallen default mode. Loving God requires a supernatural upgrade, a circumcision from the self-centeredness of our hearts (Moses). The more we truly love God, the freer we become to do "whatever we will" (Augustine), because loving God reorders our will and affections toward the good of others. When it comes to people, we need

God to help us "increase and abound in love" (Paul) because people are "in sin" (Dostoevsky), and, therefore, often extremely difficult to love.

The Unthought

We have seen two meanings of "love"—one thin and another layered and thick. But self-worship generates another definition of love, or rather seven-billion-plus definitions. Each person, as their own sovereign meaning-maker, pours their own meaning into the word "love." Here we find the redefinition most often assumed in the "love is love" hashtag, brandished across many media feeds, protest signs, and car bumpers.

This self-worshiper's redefinition of love is an example of what philosophers call an "unthought."[15] An unthought is an assumption we don't reason *to* so much as we reason *from*. The great postmodern novelist David Foster Wallace captured the idea well with a story of two young fish. They cross paths with an older fish who bids them good morning and asks, "How's the water?" Wallace narrates: "The two young fish swim on for a bit, and then eventually one of them looks over at the other and goes, 'What the hell is water?'"[16]

The fishbowl of Western culture is filled with unthoughts about love. These unthoughts are as invisible and unquestioned for us as water is for fish. So let's question the water. Perhaps its contents have something to do with the many fellow fish that are going belly up. What we might call "The Great Unthought" is the notion that, because we are each sovereign meaning-makers, love requires unquestioning endorsement of someone else's lifestyle and beliefs. To truly love someone, you must celebrate their desires and dreams or be branded with a scarlet *B* for bigot. Logically, the dogmas of self-worship—that human feelings are unfallen and unquestionable—demand this redefinition of love.

To see this unthought at work today, we may ask, "Why has the Southern Poverty Law Center affixed the label of 'hate group' to organizations like Alliance Defending Freedom, the Pacific Justice Institute, and even the American College of Pediatrics?"[17] It's simple. Such groups dare to disagree with the sexual dogmas of the SPLC. It is inconceivable that such groups disagree because they have reasonable counterpoints, or that they actually love people who live differently. No. Given the power of the Great Unthought, hate *must* be their motivation.

The Unthought has made its way into the church. Almost half of Christian millennials "agree at least somewhat that it is wrong to share one's personal beliefs with someone of a different faith in hopes that they will one day share the same faith."[18] Millennials are two times more likely than Gen X and three times more likely than boomers and elders to believe that "disagreement means judgment."[19] If it is wrong to seek the conversion of non-Christians, if disagreeing with their rejection of the gospel is too judgmental, then the Great Commission is reduced to the Not-So-Great Suggestion. We end up with a generation of Christians dutifully strapping muzzles over their mouths rather than unabashedly sharing the best news in the universe. Moreover, many have been duped into believing that such self-muzzling—depriving people of God's joyous solution to their sin problem—is somehow loving.[20]

Thinking through the Unthought

How might we debunk the Great Unthought? We debunk it the same as we would debunk any other assumption. We take away its privileged status as an unthought by, well, thinking about it. We subject it to the same standards of evidence and questioning as any other belief.

Does the Unthought make true tolerance impossible? Tolerance means treating people with respect *even when you disagree*. A Lakers fan and a Celtics fan disagree on which team is superior. Therefore, they can be truly tolerant of each other. Two Lakers fans, however, can't be *tolerant* of each other's viewpoint on the superior team because they *agree*. Agreement is different from tolerance.

Does the Unthought offer us an unrealistic vision of love? I love my wife and my wife loves me. If she finds me napping instead of mowing the lawn, I don't expect her to slow-clap me as I lay sprawled and snoring on the couch. I wouldn't celebrate if I found that she spent an inordinate amount of cash on some fancy face cream allegedly made from petrified tree bark and mythical juju berries harvested by Maori tribesmen deep in the New Zealand forest. She and I don't cheer when our kids yell, flick boogers, or elbow-drop one another. There is no shortage of disagreement in the Williams household. And yet, miracle of miracles, we still love each other! Yes, sexuality is different and far more significant than napping, splurging, and booger-flicking. But the point remains: In what fantasy land does loving someone require unwavering agreement and celebration of all their choices? Think of those you care about. If another person or group of people are demanding that you agree with them unquestioningly about everything, then they are not inviting you into a relationship but into a regime or cult.

Is the Unthought applied by a double standard? Disagreeing with Christian beliefs and mocking a Christian lifestyle are commonplace for many who champion the Unthought. If it were consistently applied, we must conclude that this failure to agree with and celebrate Christian identity is nothing but bigotry, hate, and Christian-a-phobia.

Can the Unthought be used as a form of bullying? Christians believe we are adopted children of God. This is a sincere belief at the core of a Christian identity. Imagine that Christians demanded that non-Christians address them as "Adopted Children of the

Only True God." Anyone who failed to do so could be accused of hatefully seeking to erase our existence. Any group that failed to celebrate our identity as adopted children of God would be labeled a hate group.

Demanding that Muslims, Buddhists, and atheists address Christians as such would be a form of worldview bullying. A non-Christian might respond, "You may believe those things to be true about yourself. But I don't share your worldview. You have no right to tacitly force your beliefs on me by demanding I use your words your way under threat of being called names or ostracized from society. That's not loving." The non-Christian would be right to say so. Such coercion is incompatible with a Christian view of loving our neighbors.

It is precisely this form of coercion that lies behind much of the #loveislove-inspired legislation facing schools, businesses, churches, synagogues, and mosques. Such legislation is dripping with dogma.[21] It seeks to enshrine as law certain doctrinal beliefs about the nonsupremacy of God, human unfallenness, and the sacred status of human feelings.[22] But these doctrines make sense only within certain worldviews, like the critical theory of Herbert Marcuse, the social constructionism of John Money, or the queer theory of Judith Butler—worldviews that billions of people do not embrace.

Don't be fooled by marketing slogans like #loveislove. As Alisa Childers put it, "We need to get the Disney/Kenny Rogers/eighties rom-com type of love out of our heads. True biblical love is neither a trite affirmation of someone's life choices nor holding someone hostage to our own politics."[23] What is now unfolding politically in the West is not a face-off between fundamentalist religious theocrats and freedom-loving secularists who seek a religiously neutral state that upholds all lifestyles equally. What we are seeing is nothing less than a new theocracy. There is a fundamentalist faith working to silence all heretics and enshrine itself as the only legal faith of the land. It is a faith in which the creature, not the Creator, defines the human *telos*. It is a faith with no holy God as a pride-deflating reference point to realistically assess our own fallibility.

> There is a fundamentalist faith seeking to silence all heretics and enshrine itself as the only legal faith of the land.

It is a faith that projects all evil from our own hearts onto any institution that refuses to celebrate our autonomous identities. It is a faith striving to usher in a new heaven and a new earth, centered not on Christ but on the self. It is a faith guided not by Saint Paul or Saint Peter but by Saint Marx and Saint Marcuse. Make no mistake, it is a faith.

Given the power of the Great Unthought, it is inconceivable that Christians, Jews, or Muslims who don't embrace today's trending sexual orthodoxies may truly love their neighbors. It is impossible that Christians have a sincere, defensible belief that gender distinctions are something more profound than an arbitrary social construct and that we can't erase male-female distinctions without losing something precious, beautiful, and life-giving. "No," demands the Unthought, "it *must* be bigotry, phobia, or hatred"—a rather bigoted, hateful, and phobic conclusion to draw about billions of people. And so, in the twenty-first century, we find ourselves trapped in *1984*, where 2 + 2 = 5, where war is peace, freedom is slavery, and ignorance is strength, where, we might add, actual bigotry, hate, and phobia are love.

A Dialogue with Foucault

Michel Foucault, who we met in earlier chapters, was one of the most influential thinkers to pour the ideological concrete upon which the Great Unthought stands. In his version, tipping his cap to Nietzsche, everything is about power. Thus, if someone objects to someone else's sexual lifestyle, the only possible explanation is that they are trying to wield the oppressive power of "heteronormativity." To see whether Foucault's thesis checks out, let us imagine a dialogue between Foucault and myself. If I could time travel and speak with him before his untimely death from AIDS in 1984, these are some things I would want to ask and share:

Interior. A posh San Francisco café at night.

Me: I have read up on your thinking about human sexuality.

Foucault: Great. What did you think?

Me: I'd like to test some of your conclusions right now if you don't mind.

Foucault: Have at it.

Me: Truth be told, I'm more interested in you as a person—a fellow human being—than your philosophical musings about sexuality. But perhaps we can tie the two together.

Foucault: OK, I'm interested.

Me: Your philosophy says that heterosexuality has been historically and remains a power structure. It is upheld to oppress people with what we might call nonheterosexual desires.

Foucault: Close enough.

Me: Do you count yourself among those with nonheterosexual desires?

Foucault: You know I do. There was a time, in my younger student days at Lycée Henri-IV in Paris in the late 1940s, when I first began to explore my sexuality in whatever hidden establishments the City of Love had to offer. I did feel shame, so much so I would cut myself. Mind you, there was no such thing as gay pride back in those days. My sexuality was still criminal under French law back then. I even had some power-tripping French psychiatrist diagnose me with a classic case of "homosexuality." But I'm in a much better place now.

Me: And where is that?

Foucault: San Francisco.

Me: How is that better?

Foucault: It's a city that actively resists the domination and oppression of the heterosexual majority. I can be more truly myself here.

Me: How so?

Foucault: When I arrived in San Francisco to teach at Berkeley back in 1975, I could not have been happier. I found one of the most sexually liberated communities on planet earth.

Me: What kind of "sexual liberty" did you experience there?

Foucault: You name it. In clubs like the Boot Camp, the Brig, and the Barracks, I had options for sadomasochistic sex whenever I wanted.

Me: What's that?

Foucault: You know, gagging, piercing, cutting, electric-shocking, stretching on racks, imprisoning, branding, that kind of thing. I love it, I love it all. I'm all in. I've even built myself a pretty respectable collection of clamps, handcuffs, hoods, gags, whips, and paddles.

Me: Hmmm. It seems like what you call sexual "liberty" is, literally, sexual bondage. In volume 1 of *The History of Sexuality*, you talk about what you call

"The Faustian pact . . . to exchange life in its entirety for sex itself, for the truth and the sovereignty of sex. Sex is worth dying for." Do you really believe that?

Foucault: I not only believe it, I *live* it.

Me: Do you think living that is sustainable? One of your heroes whose funeral you attended, Jean-Paul Sartre, indulged his sexual desires with a kind of reckless abandon too. He reported that the sexual rushes became less and less thrilling and, by his own admission, ended up "empty," trying to fill that emptiness with a steady stream of vodka and a milelong trail of abandoned partners.

Foucault: So what! I'm not Sartre. I've surpassed him, just like I believe I have surpassed the great sexual revolutionary Marquis de Sade, who didn't take sexual gratification far enough.

Me: What do you have to say to those who disagree with the sexual lifestyle you promote?

Foucault: I'd say that they're oppressive. Maybe they don't realize it or they're lying to themselves, but they just want more power and privilege. They think that by lording their sexual norms over me and the rest of society, and demonizing people who live like me, they can hold on to that power. I think they're pathetic. They have hate and fear in their hearts.

Me: Let me ask you this. Use your imagination with me. What if just a few decades from now virtually every major university, every major media outlet, the world's biggest corporations, the most powerful entertainers and athletes, multi-million-dollar motion pictures, children's schooling and programming, the White House, most of Congress, the United Nations, and even many churches came to embrace your beliefs about sex? What if people who failed to embrace those beliefs were called slurs daily, fired from their jobs, dragged to court, excluded from leadership positions, openly mocked, denied their freedoms to form, maintain, and publicly express their own beliefs about sexuality, punished if they fail to echo the orthodoxies of those in power?

Foucault: So what? Sounds good to me.

Me: Sure it does. But don't all those institutions flexing their power to enforce their way of thinking about human sexuality and seeking to marginalize and stigmatize everyone else sound familiar? I mean isn't that, by your own standards, precisely the kind of oppression and power grab you've spent your career fighting?

Foucault: [Looking somewhat annoyed.]

Me: Let me be frank with you, Michel. I don't hate you. I'm not afraid of you. I have zero desire to oppress or lord over you. I love you. Because I love you, I want to be honest with you. I believe you were created, with that brilliant mind of yours, for far more than what the Boot Camp, the Brig, and the Barracks are offering you. I believe that the ten million most wild sexual rushes you could imagine are nothing compared to the meaning you could find in a relationship with your Creator. I believe Jesus wants to redeem you and show you true fulfillment, the kind that lasts forever. Unlike many of your anonymous partners, he knows you by name, Michel, and numbers the hairs on your head.

Foucault: Anyone could number the hairs on my head. It's zero!

Me: *Touché.* But in all seriousness, Michel, I believe that you're settling for something far less than the eternal joy offered to you in Jesus Christ. I believe you are letting your sexual desires define you in a way that isn't good for you. I believe that confusing your core identity with your sexual wants ultimately demeans you and drastically underestimates your real value. It makes you a slave, not just to your leather-clad partners but also to yourself. You may not believe it, but you are an image-bearer of God. You were created to know and enjoy your Creator. You have no idea how desperately I want that for you, Michel. Do you think that means I hate you or fear you?

Foucault: I still think you're complicit with an oppressive system of heteronormativity trying to lord its power over me.

Me: I don't want to lord anything over you, Michel. Jesus wants to be your Lord. I promise you he is worth leaving your world of sin behind. I invite you to repent, not because I'm some hateful, raving bigot but because I love you and want you to flourish. I don't want you to realize too late that, for all of your philosophical accolades and all of your sexual escapades, you missed out on the most everlasting joy a human being can experience.

Foucault: [Looks a bit dumbfounded. Has a brief coughing fit, shakes hands firmly, and exits into the night.][24]

A Heretic's Plea

How many have been tragically duped by the Great Unthought Foucault promoted? You can truly love someone and still disagree with them. You may disagree not *in spite of* but precisely *because of* your love for them. Of course, there are myriad ways to disagree unlovingly and belittle the humanity of others from a place of hatred and fear. We have all done so. But jumping from that premise to the conclusion that disagreement equals hate is an irrational leap of faith.

One reason many are willing to take that leap is that, on the surface, #loveislove sounds, well, loving. Why not accept and celebrate everyone's love lives as equally valid? It is precisely this attitude that makes real unconditional and redemptive love impossible, impossible to both give and receive.

Take four biblical images—God loves us like a potter, shepherd, father, and groom. Now impose the Unthought on each scenario. A potter *loves* his lump of clay so much he just smiles and gives it a pat. There is no painstaking process of forming the clay into something more. The shepherd *loves* his sheep so much he lets them be their true selves, roaming wild, eating garbage, and tangling themselves in brambles. A father *loves* his son so much that he never bothers to cast a noble vision for a life of moral bravery. A groom *loves* his bride so much he foots the bill for her to chug champagne all day and never lift a finger except to buy name brands online.

The word "loves" becomes ridiculous in each scenario. Just as our culture has misnamed arrogance as authenticity, we have also mistaken apathy and a polite, unquestioning acceptance for true love. Because God is the greatest Potter, Shepherd, Father, and Lover we will ever know, he aims his divine attributes not at *affirming* but *transforming* us. Love doesn't say flatly, "Be who you already are." It says redemptively, "*Become* who you are made to be." Self-worship not only robs us of awe, originality, freedom, authenticity, humility, courage, and adventure; it also strips us of the joyous capacity to give and receive a love that is truly redemptive, like God's love.

In closing, I ask you—no, I *plead* with you—to become a heretic. Don't be a cow, mooing obediently with the herd, or a chump following all the hashtag propaganda. Brazenly reject the dogmas of our day. Boldly break the ten commandments of self-worship. If I may end where we began, with the wisdom of a nine-year-old—don't follow your heart. Your heart is fallen. Follow God's heart. "It's way better!"

A Heretic's Testimonial

Walt Heyer runs a ministry (www.waltheyer.com) to bring love, understanding, and the good news of Jesus to bear on the lives of those struggling with their gender identities. He is also a heretic against the cult of self-worship. He boldly breaks the #loveislove commandment. This is his story.

I lived eight years as a female named Laura Jensen after undergoing gender reassignment surgery. It all started when I was four years old. My grandma, a dressmaker, made me a purple chiffon dress and began showering me with praises for how wonderful I looked. Like all little kids, I craved the affirmation and attention. Many today would applaud my grandma for being so affirming, liberating her grandchild from oppressive gender stereotypes. In reality it was a seductive form of child abuse. Children are extremely pliable to adult influences about who they are. The subtle message behind such "affirmation" was that there was something wrong with me. My body was wrong. This caused massive confusion, depression, and anxiety.

Just two and a half years of cross-dressing had a profound impact on my ability to feel comfortable in my male identity, a battle that would last until I was fifty years old.

My childhood cross-dressing led to sexual abuse multiple times by my uncle. Being affirmed in a purple dress made me vulnerable and confused. The weight of being sexually abused only compounded my broken identity. When I told my parents, they said, "Oh, your uncle wouldn't do that." I was coerced into cross-dressing, endured sexual abuse, and now, apparently, I was a liar—not a good start to life.

Fast-forward to my adult self. Drinking became the tool that numbed my childhood pain, especially after getting married, fathering two children, and achieving top corporate executive positions. On the surface everything looked great, but underneath I was in unbearable angst. A therapist had the solution. "Walt, take hormones and undergo reassignment surgery." He was a world-class expert and the author of the international standards of care for treatment of gender identity disorder, but he never considered childhood sexual abuse a serious red flag. Nor did I understand how my adverse childhood experiences drove my desperation. Who was I to question him?

Overlooking early childhood sexual abuse and the psychological child abuse of cross-dressing led to the self-destructive act of turning my identity over to hormones and surgery. For eight years, with the complicity of medical professionals, I rebelled against the biological reality of my identity. I thought I had done the right thing. I thought this was cool. I thought it would solve my problems.

While working toward a PhD to help others transition

as I had, I learned more about gender dysphoria. I realized there are underlying adverse childhood experiences that no one is willing to talk about. Every single person I've worked with over the last twelve years who struggles with gender identity can identify the issue, the time, the pain, and the loss that made them not want to be who they are. Over half of them have endured sexual abuse.

Studies show up to 92 percent of children with gender dysphoria outgrow it if they aren't encouraged into gender transition by adults. Instead, self-proclaimed experts in the medical community pride themselves on injecting children with puberty blockers to interrupt their natural development, playing God with children's bodies. They cut girls' breasts off at twelve and thirteen years old, and mutilate younger and younger bodies, all in the name of "love" and "affirmation." They are manufacturing transgender kids. They manufacture depression and anxiety. Predators masquerading as pioneers of compassion are profiting from tearing young people's bodies and lives apart.

Then came the shocking moment when I studied the history of reassignment surgery and hormone treatments. It was a pseudoscience pioneered by pedophile-rights activists like Wilhelm Reich, Harry Benjamin, John Money, and Alfred Kinsey. As a transgender person, I didn't need an ideologically inspired "love" that affirmed whatever I felt. I needed people who loved me enough to gently help me see I was wrong. It was wrong for me to turn my body over to surgeons. For all his "expertise," the doctor who encouraged me toward hormone therapy and reassignment surgery was wrong.

Once I confessed that I was wrong, the door of my heart

opened. The Lord Jesus saved me, and I found who I truly am in him. That point where we acknowledge we are not perfect and open ourselves to our perfect Creator—that is where real, redemptive change happens. I found freedom as Walt again. I married an incredibly beautiful, smart lady. We have been married for twenty-five years. Thank you, Jesus. We built an outreach, http://sexchangeregret.com, to help others who have realized, all too painfully, that they have been lied to. Despite that stories like mine are often suppressed or banned, there are plenty of "detransitioners" like me who have found deep joy and meaning in bucking the lies of gender ideology and living as who God made us to be.

—Walt

A Heretic's Prayer

God,

You have been engaged in intimate community among Father, Son, and Holy Spirit since before you spoke the universe into being. You didn't create out of loneliness or neediness but out of the fullness and overflowing of your love. You made us to love. But in our fallen state, it's so easy to be selfish or reduce love to a sentimental buzzword or cheap slogan. God, help us to truly love and, therefore, obey and enjoy you more profoundly each day. Cause us to increase and abound in love for one another, especially when it's difficult. Break the antilove habits of our hearts. May your love for us become the true core of our identities. May we be so marked by your love that the watching world can better recognize the true identity of Jesus. Amen.

A Heretic's Field Manual

Before moving on to the Heretic's Manifesto, do three or four of the following to sharpen your skills at violating the #loveislove commandment:

1. Read the famous love passage of 1 Corinthians 13. As you read through the list of the properties of biblical love, ask the Holy Spirit to generate each of those properties in you this week.
2. Think of the top three least loving patterns or habits in your life. Confess them to God the Father, take them to the cross of Jesus, and ask the Holy Spirit to sovereignly break those patterns.
3. 1 John 3:18 commands us to love not only with words but also with actions. Come up with three loving actions you can do today, then go do them.
4. Think of three people you love who are doing things you know are hurting them. Pray for each one by name. Then ask God to set up divine appointments during which you can lovingly call them to repentance.
5. The New Testament church is not to be marked by its slick programming but by the depth and authenticity of its love. Attend a local church this weekend. Don't enter with a consumer mentality of what you can get out of it, but with a Christlike mentality that asks, "How can I best love and serve the people around me?" Look into any service projects the church offers and get involved.

A Heretic's Manifesto

A new religion is sweeping the globe. Eighty-four percent of Americans believe that "enjoying yourself is the highest goal of life," 86 percent believe that to enjoy yourself you must "pursue the things you desire most," while 91 percent affirm the statement: "To find yourself, look within yourself."[1] This cult of self-worship . . .

1. . . . promises our most awesome life, but robs us of awe.
2. . . . markets itself as cutting-edge, but is hopelessly outdated.
3. . . . commands us to follow our hearts, but our hearts are divided and depraved.
4. . . . encourages us to be true to ourselves, but makes us unwitting devotees to miserable men.
5. . . . tells us to be our own moral masters, but strips us of courage and credibility.
6. . . . calls us to the rush of unfettered experience and adventure, but becomes impossibly dull.
7. . . . tells us the answers are within, but that's where the problems are.
8. . . . beckons us to be authentic, but makes us arrogant.
9. . . . claims we can break the structure of reality, but reality breaks us back.
10. . . . advertises itself as loving, but makes bigots and haters of us all.

We, the undersigned, seek to be heretics against the self-worship that permeates and corrodes society. We refuse to march like good little cows when advertisers, pop stars, social media influencers, university professors, and animated animals push the dogmas of self-worship. We seek to actively subvert the religious narcissism of our day by living lives marked by . . .

1. . . . awe for the God of the Bible.
2. . . . rejection of the ancient serpent's lie to define our own reality.
3. . . . following God's heart before our own hearts.
4. . . . rebellion against the doomed philosophies of self-worship ideologues.
5. . . . courage to champion the objectively beautiful, good, and true over and against the ugliness, evil, and falsehoods of the age.
6. . . . ascending the adventurous terrain of seeking God's kingdom, rather than wandering the flatlands of our own subjectivity.
7. . . . looking to God's Word rather than within ourselves for answers.
8. . . . authenticity before the fact that God is God and we are not.
9. . . . expressing our God-given freedoms within the God-given forms of moral reality.
10. . . . loving others redemptively, with an eye toward their temporal flourishing and eternal good.

We, the undersigned, cannot live a single one of these resolutions without the help of the triune God. We, therefore, ask for a supernatural dose of his divine power and grace to live our lives to glorify the Father, the Son, and the Holy Spirit rather than the false gods of Me, Myself, and I.

Soli Deo Gloria.

Join the Heretics

Visit www.jointheheretics.com to join the redemptive revolt against self-worship for the glory of God.

Original Signatories

Holland Williams

Thaddeus Williams

Jocelyn Williams

Sean McDowell

J. P. Moreland

Alisa Childers

David Dockery

Douglas Groothuis

Erik Thoennes

Michael Horton

Josiah Solis

Howard Ahmanson

Nicole Otto

Patti Snyder

Heidi Jane Reed

Shenny Del Cid Tettleton

Brandi O'Neal

Kristen Carmitchel

Jennifer Mackey Olson

Theresa Triola

Mary Beth

Brenda Dell

Brooke Holmes

Colton Jones

Owen Runk

Amber Neill Parker

Tony McCullough

Diane Christine

Elisabeth Rhodes Owen

Mary Tabor

Olivia Sanchez

Beth Daghfal

Elle Coursey

Stacy Melton Huff

Helen Smith

Kaylynne Klimek

Christina MacDonald

Monica Menschner

Kristen Cable Wright

Joel Hernandez

Alicia Keeling Moss

Kelly Hayo Mederich

Megan Thomas

Twyla McDougall

Eric Bjerke Sr.

Erin McDill Weeks

Daniel Cieslar

Suda Sukaram Farnsworth

Sarah Benest

Tim Thetford

Jan Meyers

Marti Patterson

Kendra Carper

Lynn Nolt Rohal

Melanie Owens McFarland

Anica Rae Marcum

Jennifer Pierpont
Eve Pierce
Renee Webb Sproles
Erica Allender
Kori Champagne Glentzer
Nancy Faye
Cyndi Fish Davis
Amanda Yarbrough
Erin Prijatelj
Karen Cheney
Lauren Hunt Stephenson
Irene O'Neill
Sherry Dennis
Kimberly Joner
Elizabeth Duncan Salley
Brooke Craig
Gloria Hegarty
Liezel Pieters
Cynthia Shone
Barrack Ongaro
Jennifer Hayes Yates
John A. Bloom
Karen Smeltzer Broce
Arla Fivash Philippbar
Daisy Whisenant
Paul Murray
Danielle Coster Costa
Ben Carmona
Lindsay Carmona
Steve Doane
Tim Sherlock Sr.
Eddie Byun

Benjamin Shin
Richard Klaus
Brian Mattson
Daniel Pelichowski
Angelina Davis
Jennifer Lincoln Hanson
Susan Leonard
Margie Moore
Seth A. MacDonald
Kristy Sims Lindsay
Chuck McWhirter
Kevin Briggins
Benjamin Blowers
Bec Andrew
Allison Wardrip
Russell Williams
Judy Williams
Kathy Head
Charles Stanley
Mark Barr
Michelle Bunn
Charles Hoke
Liz Hancock
Ben Minch
Tyler Henry
Jocelyn Floyd
Taylor Alexander Brazil
Jill Bedell
Daniel Wallace
Joshua Kazas
Jon Kari
Dan Marks

Matt Jones

Stephanie Jackson

Chris Jackson

Chace Steeves

Elissa Harrell

Dana Dill

Karen Johnson

Joy Rivera

Jen Mleczynski

Josh Carey

Andrea Crum

Amber Ridgeway

Paul Frala

Dave Silvernail

Ryan Zeulner

Regina Sherlock

Darin Gerdes

Lee Nauman

Julie Spike

Kelli Marsh

James George

Christian Barnes

Janelle Robinson Sherod

Amy Kral

Chris Middleton

Julie Smyth

Mary Narvaez-Walker

Kristin Hall

Rachel Ni Chonarain

Kim Griffin Livesay

Tamara Robbins

Jan Smalley Perrigin

Amy Baggett Windham

Judith McFarland

Jeniffer DeFrates

Katie Julien

Christine Smith

Sara Cocchini

Karen Patrick

Teasi Cannon

Diana Rogers

Cheri Jones

Heather Owen

David Tienken

Marna Graham

Jennifer Schwartz

Cindy Nash Youngers

Susan Matthews

Erin MacDonald

Kevin Lewis

David Chung

Suresh Budhaprithi

Thaddeus Budhaprithi

Madhu Budhaprithi

Bill Medina

Alice Medina

Caryl Johnson

Erin Hoover

Laurie Hetherington

Tiffany Bird

Sarah Malcangi

Lewis Waha

Madison Sanchez

Thaddeus M. Maharaj

Chris Kiiskinen

Scott Palmer

Mac Morrissey

Andrea Bowen

Hunter Baker

John Appleton

Chris Bate

Brixie Mandal

Rebecca Gray Jordan

Robert MacElderry

Brad Watts

John Livingston

Donna Harris

Karen Gerharter-Goodman

Connor McGettigan

Vicki Boutwell

Curtis Hendrick

Amanda Lachmann Jones

Stan Goss

Mark Atwater

Jay Bennett

Don Plum

Jeanette Hagen Pifer

Joshua T. Rex

Thom Goldstein

Greg Ferreri

Mike Moses

Scott Jacobsen

Jordan Wright

Sherridon Sweeney

Regina Wright

Kyle Kledzik

Lynne Moody Johnson

Olin Giles

Brooke Lambkin

Jonathan Chechile

Michael Jahosky

Derek Head

John Gilson

David Wolcott

Richard Eng

Jessica Shannon Person

Tim Elliot

John Crooks

Clayton Wood

Gary Cass

Laura Keeney

Tristan Miller Ertel

Julie Klose

Heather Ham

Rick McCleary

Ashley Vallicot

Nelly Ruehl

Cathy Sheets

Carrie Sutorius Edwards

Susan Lundy Dutton

Cassie Troja

Monica Alvarado LoCorriere

Deanna Monzon

Gheorghe Rosca Jr.

Leah Beth Carroll

Kyle Venberg

Beckie Betcha

Eric Oldenburg

Lyssa Hurst

Jeremiah Holden

Tamra Molnar Chapman

Gabriel Louise Mozell

Oscar Navarro

Kelli Navarro

Acknowledgments

My thanks to Radiohead, the Police, Creedance, Arcade Fire, Elbow, Jose Gonzalez, King Gizzard and the Lizard Wizard, Roy Buchanan, and Mozart for providing my soundtrack throughout the writing process. This book would not have been possible without close friends whose general goofballery combined with reverence for God have helped me take myself far less and God far more seriously—Joe Mellema, Josiah Solis, Trevor Wright, Uche Anizor, Colton Jones, Aron McKay, John Perkins, J. P. Moreland, Sean Maroney, Ben Carmona, Brian Costanzo, and Monique Duson.

My young, mushy faith was galvanized with the works of Josh McDowell, Joni Eareckson Tada, and J. P. Moreland. To have them share their stories here is a dream come true, #livethedream. My other contributors—Alisa, Walt, Jamal, Alyssa, Trevor, David, Oscar, and Kelly—I'm grateful for the way that each of you, in your own way, proved to be what N. T. Wright calls "angled mirrors," sharing your stories by reflecting outward the glory of God to our readers.

My high-integrity bosses at Biola University and Talbot School of Theology—Erik Thoennes, Doug Huffman, Scott Rae, and Clint Arnold generously conspired to grant me a Spring 2022 research sabbatical so this book could happen. Thank you. To Ryan Pazdur at Zondervan, thank you for seeing the potential in this project, encouraging me along, and entrusting me with so much creative freedom. Emily Voss and Kim Tanner, working with you both on another project has been a joy. Taylor Landry, "in the absence of any indicators to the contrary," you, yet again, helped turn my often absurd and verbose prose into something worth reading. To my ever supportive parents, thank you for raising me not to follow my heart but to follow God's. To Jocelyn, my bride, words fall short. To Gracie, Dutch, Harlow, and Henry, thank you for all the love, insight, and comic relief. May you each grow to be formidable heretics against the cult of self-worship, for the glory of God.

Notes

Introduction: A Misfit's Guide to Sinning Boldly

1. Richard Dawkins, *The God Delusion* (Boston: MA: Mariner, 2008), 1.
2. This and the next few quotes are from "The End of Absolutes: America's New Moral Code," Barna, May 25, 2016, https://www .barna.com/research/the-end-of-absolutes-americas-new-moral -code/. This is not new. Back in 1831, Alexis de Tocqueville made the transatlantic voyage to research his celebrated opus *Democracy in America*. What he found was "an innumerable multitude of men constantly circling around in the pursuit of petty and banal pleasures with which they glut their souls. Each one of them, withdrawn into himself, is almost unaware of the fate of the rest. He touches them but feels nothing. He exists in and for Himself"; *Democracy in America*, tr. Henry Reeve, ed. Bruce Frohnen (Washington, DC: Regnery, 2002), 268.
3. Roxette, "Listen to Your Heart," MP3 audio, track 1 on the *Listen to Your Heart / Half a Woman, Half a Shadow*, EMI Electrola, 1988.
4. Reba McEntire and Vince Gill, "The Heart Won't Lie," MP3 audio, track 5 on *It's Your Call*, MCA, 1992.
5. The Kinks, "Trust Your Heart," track 9 on *Misfits*, Arista, 1978.
6. Motörhead, "Listen to Your Heart," track 11 on *Overnight Sensation*, SPV/Steamhammer, 1996.
7. Stevie Wonder and 98 Degrees, "True to Your Heart," MP3 audio, track 5 on *Mulan Movie Soundtrack*, UMG, 1998.
8. Gino Conforti, "Follow Your Heart," track 2 on *Thumbelina: Original Motion Picture Soundtrack*, SBK/EMI Records, 1994.
9. JoJo Siwa, "Nobody Can Change Me," MP3 audio, track 7 on *The J Team (Original Motion Picture Soundtrack)*, Nickelodeon, 2021.
10. These commandments come with their own liturgies, daily rituals to move the doctrines of self-worship from our heads to our hearts and hands. These include filtered social media image–crafting and filterless stream-of-consciousness public journaling, streaming service–bingeing, the on-demand gratification of pornography, and self-expressive shopping.

Chapter 1: #liveyourbestlife

1. These words are attributed to Ralph Waldo Emerson in multiple works, including the Unitarian Universalist Hymnal, although their original source, possibly Emerson's journals, has not been determined.
2. That book was *Reflect: Becoming Yourself by Mirroring the Greatest Person in History* (Bellingham, WA: Lexham, 2018).
3. Albert Einstein, *Einstein on Politics: His Private Thoughts and Public Stands*, ed. David Rowe and Robert Schulmann (Princeton, NJ: Princeton University Press, 2013), 229.
4. Einstein, *Einstein on Politics*, 229.
5. Einstein, *Einstein on Politics*, 229.
6. Arizona State behavioral scientist Michelle Shiota asks, "Why do people spend huge amounts of time, effort, and money on these apparently pointless activities," especially when "they offer neither material nor social reward?" Michelle Lani Shiota, "How Awe Sharpens Our Brains," *Greater Good*, May 11, 2016, https:// greatergood.berkeley.edu/article/item/how_awe_sharpens _our_brains.
7. Psychologist Barry Schwartz captures the irony of our age: "We have more choice, and thus more control, than people have ever had before. . . . [This] might lead you to expect that depression is going the way of polio, with autonomy and choice as the psychological vaccines. Instead, we are experiencing depression in epidemic numbers"; Barry Schwartz, *The Paradox of Choice: Why Less is More* (New York: HarperCollins, 2005), 109–110.
8. Kevin Corcoran, "Happiness on the Brain: The Neuroscience of Happiness, Part 1," *The Table*, October 21, 2015, https://cct.biola .edu/happiness-on-the-brain-neuroscience-happiness-part-1/.
9. Says Piff,

> Our investigation indicates that awe, although often fleeting and hard to describe, serves a vital social function. By diminishing the emphasis on the individual self, awe may encourage people to forgo strict self-interest to improve the welfare of others. When experiencing awe, you may not, egocentrically speaking, feel like you're at the center of the

world anymore. By shifting attention toward larger enti-
ties and diminishing the emphasis on the individual self,
we reasoned that awe would trigger tendencies to engage
in prosocial behaviors that may be costly for you but that
benefit and help others.

Piff concludes, "Might awe cause people to become more invested
in the greater good, giving more to charity, volunteering to help
others, or doing more to lessen their impact on the environment?
Our research would suggest that the answer is yes"; Paul Piff, Pia
Dietze, Matthew Feinberg, Daniel Stancato, Dacher Keltner, "Awe,
the Small Self, and Prosocial Behavior," *Journal of Personality and
Social Psychology* 108, no. 6 (2015): 883–89, https://www.apa.org
/pubs/journals/releases/psp-pspi0000018.pdf.

10. Shiota, "How Awe Sharpens Our Brains."
11. Shiota's research carries massive implications into why many
    Christians fall for bad arguments, whether they be flat earth
    theory, name-it-claim-it televangelism, or newspaper theology
    conspiracies that see the book of Revelation fulfilled in every
    headline from blood moons to Russian aggression. Could our
    susceptibility have something to do with having less awe for God
    than we let on?
12. Robert Jastrow, *God and the Astronomers* (New York: Norton, 1978),
    116.
13. Abraham Joshua Heschel, *God in Search of Man: A Philosophy of
    Judaism* (New York: Noonday, 1976), 78.
14. Paul Piff, "Awe, the Small Self, and Prosocial Behavior," *Journal of
    Personality and Social Psychology* 108, no. 6 (2015): 883–89, https://
    www.apa.org/pubs/journals/releases/psp-pspi0000018.pdf.
15. This passage has occasionally been used to support Communist
    and Socialist economic ideologies. But such an interpretation is not
    only anachronistic, it is highly inaccurate. The book of Acts knows
    nothing of government-imposed wealth redistribution.
16. An interesting side note: behavioral science has found that awe
    makes people far more likely to believe in a transcendent agency
    who sustains the universe, what scientist Piercarlo Valdesolo
    describes as the "presence and power of a supernatural being."

Summing up his research, Valdesolo says, "If I throw 10 people at the Grand Canyon and ask how many come away with a secular answer and how many come away spiritual, I'd tip the scales in favor of spiritual," quoted in Jeffrey Kluger, "Why There Are No Atheists at the Grand Canyon: All It Takes Is a Little Awe to Make You Feel Religious," *Time*, November 27, 2013, http://science.time .com/2013/11/27/why-there-are-no-atheists-at-the-grand-canyon/.

17. A. W. Pink, *The Sovereignty of God* (Grand Rapids: Baker, 1979), 19–20.

18. Frederick Douglass, *The Life and Narrative of Frederick Douglass* (Monee, IL: Public Domain, 2020), 95.

19. In the words of Old Testament scholar Walter Kaiser Jr., "The 'god' of this twenty-first century often does not equal the majestic and awesome Lord of the Scriptures. Instead, the 'god' all too frequently announced today is more of an invention of our own thinking and sentimentality"; *The Majesty of God in the Old Testament* (Grand Rapids: Baker, 2007), 10.

20. James Thrower, *Western Atheism: A Short History* (Amherst, NY: Prometheus, 2000), 25.

21. In the nineteenth century, German philosopher Ludwig Feuerbach likewise argued that religion is often a matter of projecting a super-sized version of ourselves into the heavens. Theology is often just anthropology on steroids. During the 20th century, most universities followed Feuerbach's footsteps as a majority of "Theology Departments" were rebranded as "Religious Studies Departments," signaling a shift from talking about God to talking about how we, as mere humans, talk about our different God projections.

22. See A. W. Pink, *The Attributes of God* (Grand Rapids: Baker, 1987), chs. 1–2.

23. Xenophanes, fragment 23, cited in James Thrower, *Western Atheism: A Short History* (London: Pemberton, 1971), 19.

24. W. K. Clifford, *Lectures and Essays, vol. 2* (New York: MacMillan, 1901), 245.

25. Joseph Herl and Kevin Hildebrand, "How Great Thou Art," *Lutheran Service Book Companion to the Hymns*, vol. 1 (St. Louis: Concordia, 2019), 1194–1202.

26. C. S. Lewis, *Letters to Malcolm: Chiefly on Prayer* (San Diego: Harvest, 1964), 4–5.

Chapter 2: #okboomer

1. Rodney Clapp, "The Theology of Consumption and the Consumption of Theology," *The Consuming Passion: Christianity & Consumer Culture*, ed. Rodney Clapp (Downers Grove, IL: InterVarsity Press, 1998), 188.

2. Abraham Kuyper, *Common Grace: God's Gifts for a Fallen World*, vol. 1, ed. Jordan Ballor and Stephen Grabill (Bellingham, WA: Lexham, 2016), 124.

3. Some have taken "knowledge" here to mean personal knowledge as opposed to mere abstract knowledge. Before they fell into temptation, Adam and Eve could only know the difference between good and evil *theoretically*. Eating the forbidden fruit showed our first parents the difference between good and evil *by firsthand experience*, by what theologians have dubbed *cognitio experimentalis*. Adam and Eve would not only *know about* evil but would *know evil*, having perpetrated it themselves. The abstract became painfully personal. There are several problems with this reading, not the least of which is that the text says, "You will be *like God* knowing good and evil." The God of the Bible certainly doesn't know evil by *cognitio experimentalis*. He never has and never will have firsthand experience of perpetrating injustice.

4. This sense of knowing as a Maker's choosing occurs again and again in Old Testament literature. See Genesis 18:19; Psalm 1:6; Jeremiah 1:5; Hosea 13:5; Amos 3:2 in the Old Testament. New Testament examples include John 10:27 and 2 Timothy 2:19. The closest example to the Genesis fall narrative is found in Job 34:4. For an in-depth case for knowing as maker's knowledge in Genesis 3:5 see Kuyper, *Common Grace*, vol. 1, 235–44.

5. It is similar to the ancient Egyptian term "evil-good," which meant everything, or the line from Homer's *Odyssey* that says, "I know all things, the good and the evil."

6. Friedrich Nietzsche, *The Will to Power* (New York: Vintage, 1968), 550.

7. See Thaddeus Williams, *Reflect: Becoming Yourself By Mirroring the*

Greatest Person in History (Bellingham: WA, Lexham, 2018), chapter 3, "Flip."

8. As Abraham Kuyper put it, Adam . . .

> . . . decided to evaluate for himself, and came to the conclusion opposite God's conclusion, and as independent evaluator of good and evil, he placed himself over against God and through this fell away from God. He wanted to stand beside God as a second god, just as Satan had suggested. God and man this would both independently and sovereignly evaluate what was good and what was evil, and this unlocked all depths of sin. This we see exactly how it was this arbitrary probationary command of the tree of knowledge that became the effective means to bring man to the decision whether he wanted to leave to God the knowledge, that it, the assessment of good and evil or take it to himself. . . . Knowledge of good and evil means that man himself sovereignty evaluates, determines, and decides what is good and what is evil for him. (Kuyper, *Common Grace*, 240, 242)

9. Mike McPhate, "California Today: Berkeley Turns to Comedian For Advice," *New York Times*, April 11, 2017, https://www.nytimes.com /2017/04/11/us/california-today-jobrani.html.

10. Paula Abdul, "10 Ultimate Quotes from the Word's Best Musicians," Music Think Tank, retrieved February 13, 2023, https://www .musicthinktank.com/blog/10-ultimate-quotes-from-the-worlds -best-musicians.html.

11. "Cutty Sark—Follow Your Heart," BooProductionsGreece, December 2, 2019, YouTube video, 0:30, https://www.youtube.com /watch?v=n7iSzC1p6Kk.

12. "Minecraft Create Your World T-Shirt," Hot Topic, retrieved February 13, 2023, https://www.hottopic.com/product/minecraft -create-your-world-t-shirt/19557034.html.

13. Jeremy Rifkin, *Algen: A New Word—A New World* (New York: Viking, 1983), 244.

14. I have found by experience that there are essentially two ways to become an idiot. There is thinking too much and thinking that our

thinking is the final word on reality. That is called hubris. Then there is thinking too little, and thinking that our lack of thinking is some mark of great faith. That is called hysteria. Reverence for God is an illuminated path between the two.

15. RuPaul, "RuPaul on Why Identity Shouldn't Be Taken Seriously, But Loving Yourself Should," *Time*, April 19, 2017, https://time.com /4746895/rupaul-time-100-video/.

Chapter 3: #followyourheart

1. Steve Jobs, "How to Live Before You Die," Stanford University Commencement Speech, TED, retrieved February 22, 2023, https:// www.ted.com/talks/steve_jobs_how_to_live_before_you_die.

2. Anna Quindlen, "1999 Mount Holyoke Commencement Speech," James Clear, retrieved February 22, 2023, https://jamesclear.com /great-speeches/1999-mount-holyoke-commencement-speech-by -anna-quindlen.

3. David Wells describes our condition well: "The proud and erect shaper of life first remakes reality and then finds that what has been remade has no existence outside his or her private consciousness. . . . The self, now left completely to itself, cut off from God and from the outside world, began to disappear"; *No Place for Truth: Or Whatever Happened to Evangelical Theology?* (Grand Rapids: Eerdmans, 1993), 61–63.

4. David Foster Wallace, "This Is Water," commencement speech at Kenyon College, 2005, https://fs.blog/david-foster-wallace-this -is-water/.

5. Cited in Herman Bavinck, *Reformed Dogmatics: God and Creation*, vol. 2, ed. John Bolt, trans. John Vriend (Grand Rapids: Baker Academic, 2004), 123–24.

6. C. S. Lewis, *The Abolition of Man* in *The Complete Lewis Signature Classics* (New York: HarperCollins, 2007), 710.

7. *The Incredibles*, directed by Brad Bird (Burbank, CA: Buena Vista Pictures, 2004), DVD.

8. Indeed, if we really peer deeply inside, what we will find is a battlefield covered in smoke plumes, bomb craters, and barbed wire, with opposing desires, each one an imperialist, hurling grenades and trying to outflank and destroy others. Which

desires win? Which desires merit the metal of being honored as our "heart"? Which do we follow? With no standard above the sovereign self, self-worship offers no answers to these pressing questions.

9. Jean-Jacques Rousseau, *il n'y a point de perversité originelle dans le cœur humain Émile, ou De l'éducation/Édition* 1852/Livre II; *Letters to Malesherbes*, in *The Collected Writings of Rousseau*, vol. 5, ed. Christopher Kelly, Roger D. Masters, and Peter G. Stillman, trans. Christopher Kelly (Hanover, NH: University Press of New England, 1995), 575; *Oeuvres Complètes*, vol. 1, ed. Bernard Gagnebin and Marcel Raymond (Paris: Gallimard, Bibliothèque de la Pléiade, 1959–1995), 1136.

10. Joel Osteen, *Becoming a Better You: 7 Keys to Improving Your Life Every Day* (New York: Free Press, 2007), 56, 87, 91, 129. Osteen is far from alone in this conviction. The widespread belief that we are basically good has been described accurately by R. C. Sproul as "the Pelagian captivity of the church." See R. C. Sproul, "The Pelagian Captivity of the Church," *Modern Reformation* 10, no. 3 (2001): 22–9. Historically, we can trace the staggering confidence in humanity's moral abilities from Pelagius in the fourth century, to Erasmus in the sixteenth century, to Charles Finney in the nineteenth century, and even many Christian pastors in our day. In Pelagian thought, "human nature is uncorrupted, and the natural will competent to all good . . . and salvation is essentially a work of man"; Philip Schaff, *History of the Christian Church*, vol. 3 (Grand Rapids: Eerdmans, 1985), 815. For similar analysis of Pelagius's thought, see Richard Flathman, *Political Obligation* (Taylor & Francis, 1973), 36. For Erasmus, "It is in the power of every man to keep what is commanded"; *Diatribe Concerning Free Will*, cited in Martin Luther, *Bondage of the Will* (St. Louis: A Martin Luther Book, Concordia Publishing, 2012), 171. For Finney, "Men have power or ability to do all their duty"; *Finney's Systematic Theology*, 3rd ed., ed. Dennis Carroll (1878; Minneapolis: Bethany, 1994), 307.

11. Celine Dion, "If you follow your dreams, it means you follow your heart," Celine Dion noona, May 22, 2001, YouTube video, 1:17, https://www.youtube.com/watch?v=y5JiQEaQD30.

12. Marquis de Condorcet, *Sketch for a Historical Picture of the Progress*

of the Human Mind, in *Readings on Human Nature*, ed. Peter Loptson (Peterborough, Ontario: Broadview, 1998), 127.

13. Just two centuries before the secularist's reign of terror, those same Paris streets ran red during the Saint Bartholomew's Day massacre, a slaughter fest instigated by religious zealots. In 1572 droves of French Protestants (known as Huguenots) gathered in the City of Love for what was to be a jubilant wedding party for their leader Henry of Navarre, who married the king's sister. It was a trap. In a treacherous page of history that looks torn from a *Game of Thrones* novel, the French king instigated the assassination of Protestant leaders celebrating in Paris. What ensued was a bloodbath that splattered across France.

   The next century endured the Thirty Years War with over four million human casualties between 1618 and 1648. One obvious lesson we can learn from all the carnage and gore through church history is that people can use religion to do terrible things, and this sad truth serves as one powerful catalyst for secularization. Tertullian wrote back in the second century that the blood of the martyrs is the seed of the church. We could add that the blood of the heretics is the seed of secularism. Religious violence has historically been one factor that propels caring people to seek meaning beyond the blood-stained borders of institutionalized faith.

14. David Meyers, "A New Look at Pride," in *Your Better Self*, ed. C. W. Ellison (San Francisco: Harper & Row, 1983), 83.

15. Meyers, "A New Look at Pride," 90.

16. Meyers, "A New Look at Pride," 90.

17. Meyers, "A New Look at Pride," 84.

18. Michael Ruse, "Darwinism and Christianity Redux: A Response to My Critics," *Philosophia Christi* 4 (2002): 189–94, 192. Alvin Plantinga concurs, "The doctrine of original sin has been verified in the wars, cruelty, and general hatefulness that have characterized human history from its very inception to the present," *Warranted Christian Belief* (Oxford: Oxford University Press, 2000), 207.

Chapter 4: #betruetoyourself

1. Bob Dylan, "Gonna Have to Serve Somebody," MP3 audio, track 1 on *Slow Train Comin'*, Columbia, 1979.

2. Nineteen centuries earlier, the apostle Paul, like Dylan, tried to jolt people with "a knowledge of the truth [so] they may come to their senses and escape from the snare of the devil, after being captured by him to do his will" (2 Tim. 2:25–26).

3. We face what C. S. Lewis described in the late 1960s as "the fatal superstition that men can create values, that a community can choose its 'ideology' as men choose their clothes"; "The Poison of Subjectivism," in *Christian Reflections*, ed. Walter Hooper (Grand Rapids: Eerdmans, 1967), 73. In the ahead-of-its-time book, *The Invisible Religion*, sociologist Thomas Luckmann noticed this rising trend back in the 1960s. "The individual," said Luckmann, "is left to his own devices in choosing goods and services, friends, marriage partners, neighbors, hobbies and . . . even 'ultimate' meanings in a relatively autonomous fashion. The consumer orientation, in short, is not limited to economic products but characterizes the relation of the individual to the entire culture"; *The Invisible Religion* (New York: MacMillan, 1967), 98.

4. Consider, as a real-world case in point, Ellen DeGeneres's 1997 Emmy speech for her work on the historic "coming out" episode of *Ellen*: "I accept this on behalf of all people, and the teen-agers out there especially, who think there is something wrong with them because they are gay. There's nothing wrong with you. Don't ever let anybody make you feel ashamed of who you are." Philosopher Francis Beckwith called Ellen's seemingly affirming speech an example of "passive-aggressive tyranny." Beckwith explained,

> The trick is to sound "passive" and accepting of "diversity" while at the same time putting forth an aggressively partisan agenda and implying that those who disagree are not only stupid but also harmful. . . . Imagine if a conservative Christian Emmy-award winner had said, "I accept this on behalf of all people, and the teen-agers out there especially, who think there is something wrong with them because they believe that human beings are made for a purpose and that purpose includes the building of community with its foundation being heterosexual monogamy. There's nothing wrong with you. Don't ever let anybody, especially

television script writers, make you feel ashamed because of
what you believe is true about reality." Clearly this would
imply that those who affirm liberal views on sexuality are
wrong. An award winner who made this speech would be
denounced as narrow, bigoted, and intolerant. That person
could expect never again to work in Hollywood." (Francis
Beckwith, "Deconstructing Liberal Tolerance," Christian
Research Institute, June 11, 2009, https://www.equip.org
/article/deconstructing-liberal-tolerance/.)

5. The best analysis of Rousseau's thought, along with Marx and
   Nietzsche, in shaping the expressive individualism of our day
   comes from my friend and colleague Carl Trueman in his opus *The
   Rise and Triumph of the Modern Self: Cultural Amnesia, Expressive
   Individualism, and the Road to the Sexual Revolution* (Crossway,
   2020) and his follow-up *Strange New World: How Thinkers and
   Activists Redefined Identity and Sparked the Sexual Revolution*
   (Crossway, 2022).

6. Jean-Jacques Rousseau, *Confessions*, ed. Patrick Coleman, tr. Angela
   Scholar (Oxford: Oxford University Press, 2000), 5, 270.

7. Friedrich Nietzsche, *Thus Spake Zarathustra* in *The Philosophy of
   Nietszche* (New York: Random House, 1954), 18.

8. Nietzsche, *Thus Spake Zarathustra*, 24.

9. While some credit Nietzsche's insanity exclusively to his syphilis,
   many see his own philosophy as a contributing factor. MIT Press
   has published a fascinating piece from this perspective by George
   Bataille and Annette Michelson titled "Nietzsche's Madness" in the
   journal *October* (Spring 1986): 42–45, https://doi.org/10.2307/778548.

10. Michel Foucault, "Right of Death and Power over Life," Part 5, *The
    History of Sexuality*, vol. 1 (New York: Pantheon, 1978), retrieved
    February 8, 2023, https://caringlabor.wordpress.com/2010/08/06
    /michel-foucault-right-of-death-and-power-over-life/.

11. Michel Foucault, "Sexuality, Morality, and the Law," *Michel
    Foucault: Politics, Philosophy, Culture: Interviews and Other Writings*,
    tr. Alan Sheridan (New York: Routledge, 1988), retrieved July 20,
    2022, https://www.ipce.info/ipceweb/Library/danger.htm.

12. Roger Kimball, "The Perversions of M. Foucault," *The New*

Criterion, March 1993, https://newcriterion.com/issues/1993/3
/the-perversions-of-m-foucault.

13. Martin Booth, *A Majick Life: The Biography of Aleister Crowley* (London: Coronet, 2000), 125.

14. Richard Spence, *Secret Agent 666: Aleister Crowley, British Intelligence and the Occult* (Port Townsend, WA: Feral, 2008), 10.

15. Marco Pasi, *Aleister Crowley and the Temptation of Politics*, tr. Ariel Godwin (Durham: Acumen, 2014), 52–53.

16. Jean-Paul Sartre, *Existentialism from Dostoevsky to Sartre*, ed. Kaufman (New York: New American Library, 1975), 291.

17. Warren Ward, *Lovers of Philosophy: How the Intimate Lives of Seven Philosophers Shaped Modern Thought* (UK: Ockham, 2022), ch. 5.

18. Warren Ward, *Lovers of Philosophy*, ch. 5.

19. Webster Schott, "The Last Days of Jean-Paul Sartre," *Washington Post*, May 20, 1984, https://www.washingtonpost.com/archive /entertainment/books/1984/05/20/the-last-days-of-jean-paul -sartre/3f75987e-69af-43f7-a2ff-a386b7947c6c/.

20. "Tune In Turn On & Drop Out 1967," nathanolson, March 26, 2016, YouTube video, 3:38, https://www.youtube.com/watch?v =UQWyC9Z5X-8.

21. Some may respond to this point by arguing that agnosticism is, therefore, the best life path. Rather than a faith, agnosticism simply says "I don't know." It withholds a faith commitment to any option. Except that it doesn't. Agnosticism requires the belief that no worldview out there, no religious system that millions have held dear has enough proof to merit one's belief. It requires a rather bold faith that every other belief system on the market is unworthy of belief, which is hardly as humble and open-minded as the agnostic claims.

22. Nietzsche, *Beyond Good and Evil* (New York: Penguin, 1983), 176.

23. Friedrich Nietzsche, *Thus Spake Zarathustra* in *The Philosophy of Nietzsche* (New York: The Modern Library, 1954), 23–25.

Chapter 5: #youdoyou

1. Quoted in Doug Van Pelt, *Rock Stars on God: 20 Artists Speak Their Mind on Faith* (Relevant Books, 2004), 174.

2. Hans Rookmaaker, *Modern Art and the Death of Culture* (Wheaton, IL: Crossway, 1994), 27.

3. If Venus is no more, then the lute player has three basic options:

> Option 1: *He can change jobs, sell his lute, and buy a microscope.* After all, if beauty reduces to "sophistry and illusion" (Hume), then why waste your time with beauty-pursuing endeavors like art?

> Option 2: *Our artist can stick to his profession and look to the ash heap for inspiration.* This was the option taken by many artists in the modern art movement. Many tried to capture the shocking absurdity and gaping emptiness of life in a universe where beauty and love no longer hold living value. "Venus Is Dead (And Here's What the World Looks like Without Her)" would be an accurate title for a gallery show hanging Edvard Munch's *The Scream*, Picasso's *Les Demoiselles' d'Avignon*, Francis Bacon's *Head VI*, and vast warehouses of other modern artworks. But there is a third option our artist could take, an option much closer to how the cultural mainstream reacted to the death of objective values.

> Option 3: *Rather than look outside himself, where there are only ashes, he can turn within himself for inspiration.* He can abandon his mission of finding and expressing bigger-and-beyond-himself beauty and spend his time, instead, gazing inward and expressing whatever he finds within the confines of his own consciousness. The artist's own subjective feelings now become the primary subject matter. This third option is closest to the mainstream of Western cultures over the last century.

4. Jean-Paul Sartre, *Existentialism and Human Emotion* (Secaucus, NJ: Citadel, 1957), 42.

5. Richard Rorty, *Philosophy and the Mirror of Nature* (Princeton, NJ: Princeton University Press, 1979), 176.

6. "Interview with Johnny Rotten," *Daily Mirror*, 1983 in *Oxford Essential Quotations*, 6th edition, ed. Susan Ratcliffe (Oxford University Press, 2018), 29.

7. Michael Ruse, "The Evolution of Ethics," in *Religion and the Natural Sciences*, ed. J. E. Huchingson (Orlando: Harcourt Brace, 1993), 310.

8. Richard Rorty, *Achieving Our Country: Leftist Thought in Twentieth-Century America* (Cambridge, MA: Harvard University Press, 1998), 16.

9. Forge, "Gender Neutral Pronouns," retrieved on July 20, 2022, https://forge-forward.org/wp-content/uploads/2020/08/gender-neutral-pronouns1.pdf.

10. See, for example, Gregory Koukl and Francis Beckwith's *Relativism: Feet Firmly Planted in Midair,* J. Budziszewski's *What We Can't Not Know,* and C. S. Lewis's *The Abolition of Man.*

11. Frederick Douglass, *The Life and Narrative of Frederick Douglass* (Monee, IL: Public Domain, 2020), 95.

12. Ruth Benedict, *Patterns of Culture* (New York: Houghton-Mifflin, 1934), 257.

13. Relativism precludes the possibility of a culture making moral progress, since there is no metaethical reference point beyond the culture itself for it to progress toward, making intracultural critique impossible, perhaps even "immoral." In the name of global tolerance, relativism also cut us off from crosscultural moral critique so essential to courageously countering dehumanizing regimes, apartheid, the caste system, female circumcision, human trafficking, genocide, terrorism, and the like.

14. Amitabh Pal, "Shirin Ebadi Interview," *The Progressive Magazine,* September 1, 2004, https://progressive.org/magazine/helen-thomas-interview/.

15. Douglass, *The Life and Narrative of Frederick Douglass,* 95.

16. Douglass, *The Life and Narrative of Frederick Douglass,* 101.

17. The White Rose Society, "The Third Leaflet," retrieved on July 20, 2022, http://www.whiterosesociety.org/WRS_pamphets_third.html.

18. The White Rose Society, "Leaflet of Resistance," retrieved on July 20, 2022, http://www.whiterosesociety.org/WRS_pamphets_fifth.html.

19. William Wilberforce, *Real Christianity* (Minneapolis, MN: Bethany, 2006), 24.

20. "Debate on Mr. Wilberforce's Resolutions Respecting the Slave

Trade," in William Cobbett, *The Parliamentary History of England: From the Norman Conquest in 1066 to the Year 1803*, 36 vols. (London: T. Curson Hansard, 1806–1820), 28 (1789–91), cols. 42–68.

21. Relativism makes it impossible for individuals to make moral progress, since there is no standard of moral value beyond the individual rendering all moral change horizontal (different) but not vertical (better). The wife-beating alcoholic who has done the hard work of staying sober and dealing with his underlying anger issues hasn't gotten any better, morally speaking, but merely swapped moral personal visions, which is patently absurd. The same problem affixes to cultural relativism. We all know that the Germany today that does not send Jews, gypsies, homosexuals, and dissenting Christians to the concentration camps has morally progressed since the late 1930s. Again, that makes sense only if there is an objective moral standard higher than culture, in this case, Germany, which they have progressed toward.

22. The literature on relativism speaks often of the Reformer's Dilemma, the way in which it turns heroes into villains. If cultural relativism is true, then the highest moral standard that exists is culture itself. By challenging their cultures moral heroes like Martin Luther King Jr., William Wilberforce, Mother Teresa, Václav Havel turn out to be villains for violating the highest moral law that exists in a cultural relativist's worldview.

23. Sartre, *Existentialism and Human Emotion*, 22. Sartre borrowed this insight from Ivan Karamazov in Fyodor Dostoevsky's *Brothers Karamazov*.

24. As Sartre's fellow atheist Arthur Leff acknowledges, "No person, no combination of people, no document however hallowed by time, no process, no premise, nothing is equivalent to an actual God in this central function as the unexaminable examiner of good and evil. . . . The so-called death of God turns out not to have been just His funeral, it also seems to have affected the total elimination of any coherent, or even more than momentarily convincing ethical or legal system"; "Unspeakable Ethics, Unnatural Rights," *Duke Law Journal* 6 (December 1979), 1232.

Chapter 6: #yolo

1. Colin Campbell offers the best explanation of the #yolo doctrine I have yet to see in print:

> The "self" becomes, in effect, a very personal god or spirit to whom one owes obedience. Hence "experiencing," with all its connotations of gratificatory and stimulative feelings becomes an ethical activity, an aspect of duty. This is a radically different doctrine of the person, who is no longer conceived of as a "character" constructed painfully out of the unpromising raw material of original sin, but as a "self" liberated through experiences and strong feelings from the inhibiting constraints of social convention. (Quoted by Craig M. Gay in "Sensualists without Heart: Contemporary Consumerism in Light of the Modern Project," in *The Consuming Passion*, ed. Rodney Clapp [Downers Grove, IL: InterVarsity Press, 1998], 28.)

2. C. S. Lewis, *The Chronicles of Narnia: The Last Battle* (New York: HarperTrophy, 1994), 201–202.
3. Lewis, *The Last Battle*, 206–207.
4. Lewis, *The Last Battle*, 210–211.
5. Atheist Bertrand Russell faces the implication squarely: "No fire, no heroism, no intensity of thought and feeling, can preserve an individual life beyond the grave; that all labours of the ages, all the devotion, all the inspiration, all the noonday brightness of human genius, are destined to extinction in the vast death of the solar system, and the whole temple of Man's achievement must inevitably be buried beneath the debris of a universe in ruins"; *Mysticism and Logic* (London: Longman's, Green and Co., 1925), 47–48.
6. C. S. Lewis, *The Weight of Glory* (New York: HarperOne, 2001), 45–46.
7. Another way to get at the point is with the biblical term *makar*, translated "blessed" or "happy." This is something that infinite lifetimes worth of self-gratification could never achieve. *Makar* is closer to what William Wilberforce (played by Ioan Gruffudd) feels

in the closing scene of the historical drama *Amazing Grace*. After eleven years of hard questing, the good news comes: British slavery has been legally abolished! Parliamentarians rise in thunderous applause to congratulate Wilberforce for his exhausting and finally victorious efforts. *Makar* is what beams from his humbled, teary-eyed face. It is a pinnacle of happiness that the autonomous self, weighed down with all its wanting and consuming, can never attain.

8. David Foster Wallace, "This Is Water," commencement speech at Kenyon College, 2005, https://fs.blog/david-foster-wallace-this -is-water/.

Chapter 7: #theanswersarewithin

1. Rachel McRady, "Top 5 Best Christina Aguilera Songs of All Time," *Wetpaint*, April 2, 2015, https://web.archive.org/web/20150402151730 /http://www.wetpaint.com/the-voice/articles/top-5-best-christina -aguilera-songs-of-all-time.

2. Greg Lukianoff and Jonathan Haidt, *The Coddling of the American Mind: How Good Intentions and Bad Ideas are Setting a Generation Up for Failure* (New York: Penguin, 2019), 38.

3. Lukianoff and Haidt, *The Coddling of the American Mind*, 37.

4. Many scholars believe that Psalms 42 and 43 were originally a single psalm. Psalm 43 ends with the identical interrogation of his downcast soul, bringing the total to three.

5. Edward Monkton, retrieved February 6, 2023, http://www.edwardmonkton.com/.

6. Practicing the discipline of biblical CBT—and it is a discipline— can help us experience substantial healing from cognitive distortions. I borrow the term "substantial healing" from Francis Schaeffer's *True Spirituality*, in which he distinguishes between "substantial healing" and "total healing." Total healing awaits us in glory. This side of heaven we are still battered and bruised and, while we can't expect total healing yet, we can still experience substantial healing. That distinction will become more meaningful and encouraging to you the more you practice biblical CBT.

7. This doesn't happen all at once, and there are no shortcuts. Biblical CBT is a lifelong process. Some days the falsehoods may seem to

drown out truth, so give yourself plenty of grace. Surround yourself with people who affirm what God says it true about you and can remind you on days when your spiritual amnesia kicks in. And of course, participate in a local church, getting together with fellow spiritual amnesiacs who need the same reminders from God's Word and the Lord's Table that you do. By learning to meditate day and night on what God says rather than what your heart says, you find yourself on a fruitful path of the blessed life.

8. Bestselling author Francis Fukuyama points the way: "The problem is that the inner selves we are celebrating may be cruel, violent, narcissistic, or dishonest. Or they may simply be lazy and shallow"; *Identity: The Demand for Dignity and the Politics of Resentment* (New York: Farrar, Straus and Giroux, 2018).

9. As John Owen put it in his classic work, *The Mortification of Sin*, "Indwelling sin is compared to a person, a living person, called the old man. . . . This (says the apostle) must be killed, put to death, mortified; that is, have its power, life, vigor, and strength to produce its effects, taken away by the Spirit"; *The Mortification of Sin in Believers* in *Overcoming Sin and Temptation*, ed. Kelly Kapic and Justin Taylor (Wheaton, IL: Crossway, 2006), 48.

10. John Owen, *The Mortification of Sin*, 17, retrieved February 8, 2023, https://www.google.com/books/edition/Mortification_of_Sin /EhUiCwAAQBAJ?hl=en&gbpv=1.

11. J. R. R. Tolkien, "On Fairy Stories," 33, retrieved February 6, 2023, https://coolcalvary.files.wordpress.com/2018/10/on-fairy-stories1 .pdf.

Chapter 8: #authentic

1. Canadian philosopher Charles Taylor summed up this attitude well. By authenticity, Taylor said, "I mean the understanding of life which emerges with the Romantic expressivism of the late-eighteenth century, that each one of us has his/her own way of realizing our humanity, and that it is important to find and live out one's own, as against surrendering to conformity with a model imposed on us from outside, by society, or the previous generation, or religious or political authority." *A Secular Age* (Cambridge, MA: Harvard University Press, 2007), 475.

2. Yuval Levin described it well:

> That term suggests not only a desire to pursue one's own path but also a yearning for fulfillment through the definition and articulation of one's own identity. It is a drive both to be more like whatever you already are and also to live in society by fully asserting who you are. The capacity of individuals to define the terms of their own existence by defining their personal identities is increasingly equated with liberty and with the meaning of some of our basic rights, and it is given pride of place in our self-understanding. (*The Fractured Republic: Renewing America's Social Contract in an Age of Individualism* [New York: Basic, 2017].)

3. Colin Campbell quoted by Craig M. Gay in "Sensualists without Heart: Contemporary Consumerism in Light of the Modern Project," in *The Consuming Passion*, ed. Rodney Clapp (Downers Grove, IL: InterVarsity Press, 1998), 28.

4. *The Princess Bride*, directed by Rob Reiner (Los Angeles: Twentieth Century Fox, 1987).

5. Nations plotting against the Almighty is laughable, even if we are too busy fretting about political threats to see any comedy in creatures thinking they can legislate their Creator out of existence.

6. Jane Caro, "Why I Am Fine with Being Flawed and Ordinary," *Sydney Morning Herald*, July 28, 2017, https://www.smh.com.au /lifestyle/life-and-relationships/jane-caro-why-i-am-fine-with -being-flawed-and-ordinary-20170727-gxjygs.html.

7. Recounted by Ron Ratliff, "The Art of Living Well in a Time of Crisis," Benedictine College, January 4, 2012, https://media .benedictine.edu/2012/g-k-chesterton-and-the-art-of-living-well -in-a-time-of-crisis.

8. G. K. Chesterton, *Orthodoxy* (New York: John Lane Company, 1908), 223.

9. See Greg Lukianoff and Jonathan Haidt, *The Coddling of the American Mind: How Good Intentions and Bad Ideas Are Setting a Generation Up for Failure* (New York: Penguin, 2019), ch. 7. I am not arguing that shifting the weight of self-making from the Creator to the creature's shoulders is the exclusive factor in these unnerving

statistics. But if we take seriously Paul's Romans 1 argument about the disarray that ensues from creation worship, then we would be missing something profound if we limit ourselves to a sociological (at the exclusion of a spiritual) account of our present brokenness.

10. Idina Menzel, "Let It Go," MP3, track 10 on *Frozen: Original Motion Picture Soundtrack* (Walt Disney/Wonderland Music Company, 2014).

11. Daniel Ingram, "Time to Be Awesome," MP3, track 3 on *My Little Pony: The Movie Soundtrack*, (Nashville: RCA, 2017).

12. Jean-Paul Sartre, cited by Francis Schaeffer, *Pollution and the Death of Man* (Wheaton, IL: Crossway, 1992), 89.

13. David Foster Wallace, "This Is Water."

14. See also Deuteronomy 32:6.

Chapter 9: #livethedream

1. Walt Disney himself is often credited with these words, though he likely never said them. They likely originate from Imagineer Tom Fitzgerald. See David, "Did Walt Disney Ever Say the 'If You Can Dream It, You Can Do It' Quote?", *Notes from Neverland*, January 3, 2022, https://notesfromneverland.com/disney-info/did-walt-disney -ever-say-the-if-you-can-dream-it-you-can-do-it-quote/.

2. Ilene Woods, "A Dream Is a Wish Your Heart Makes," MP3, *Cinderella Soundtrack*, RCA/EMI, 1950.

3. There is a viral clip from *Three Miles North of Molkom* in which a ponytailed guru trains his students how to harness their psychic energy to fend off attacks with a self-generated force field. It's the kind of clip you can't help laughing at even though you know you probably shouldn't. A brunette woman harnesses all the universe's energy to create her force field as the guru charges toward her full speed. Rather than being repelled by her powerful psyche, the guru flattens the poor woman. She squirms in agony on the ground. The rules of reality cannot be believed out of existence, and if we don't acknowledge them, they will clobber us.

4. "O LORD . . . Why does the way of the wicked prosper" (Jer. 12:1)?

5. Dylan Matthews, "9 Questions about Furries You Were Too Embarrassed to Ask," *Vox*, March 27, 2015, https://www.vox.com /2014/12/10/7362321/9-questions-about-furries-you-were-too -embarrassed-to-ask.

6. As Francis Schaeffer noted, "Perhaps you remember one of Godard's movies, *Pierrot le Fou*, in which he has people going out through the windows, instead of through the doors. But the interesting thing is that they do not go out through the solid wall"; *He Is There and He Is Not Silent* (Wheaton, IL: Tyndale, 2001), 5. For a brilliant analysis of the consequences of breaking the givenness of reality's structure, see J. Budziszewksi's *What We Can't Not Know: A Guide* (San Francisco: Ignatius, 2003).

7. *Small Potatoes*, Season 1, Episode 20, "I Just Want to be Me," directed by Josh Selig, aired May 19, 2011, on Disney Jr., https://www.youtube.com/watch?v=VzJkrYxcnTk.

8. *Small Potatoes*, season 1, episode 21, "We're All Just Potatoes at Heart," directed by Josh Selig, aired May 20, 2011, on Disney Jr., https://www.youtube.com/watch?v=Ukf7oxWbQBQ.

9. Jean-Paul Sartre, *Existentialism and Human Emotion* (Secaucus, NJ: Citadel, 1957), 22.

10. What was that the Lord said about it being better to have a millstone tethered to your neck and be cast into the sea than to lead little ones astray?

11. "Bo Burnham's Inspirational Advice: Give Up Now," Conan on TBS, January 26, 2018, https://www.youtube.com/watch?v=q-JgG0ECp2U.

12. "Probability of Competing beyond High School," NCAA, retrieved on July 20, 2022, https://www.ncaa.org/sports/2013/12/17/probability-of-competing-beyond-high-school.aspx.

13. "Animatronic Ursula Loses Head in Front of 'Little Mermaid' Riders at Disney's California Adventure," KTLA 5, January 30, 2018, https://ktla.com/news/local-news/disneyland-ursula-loses-head-terrifies-everyone/.

14. See 2 Thess. 1:9–10; Rev. 21:23; John 17:24; Ps. 76:10; Prov. 16:4; Jn. 4:34; 7:18; 12:27–28; 17:4; Phil. 2:5–11; John 16:7–15; Eph. 1:13–14; Eph. 1:3–14; Rom. 9:22–24; and Rom. 11:36.

Chapter 10: #loveislove

1. "Dystopian" is the opposite of "utopian." A "utopia" is a good (Greek: *eu*) place (Greek: *topos*). A "dystopia" is a bad place. Dystopian literature explores how humans, in all our shortsightedness and hubris, make bad places.

2. Ray Bradbury, *Fahrenheit 451* (New York: Simon & Schuster, 2003), 58.

3. "Suggested Language List," Brandeis, retrieved on July 20, 2022, https://sites.google.com/brandeis.edu/parcsuggestedlanguagelist /categories.

4. "Suggested Language List."

5. C. S. Lewis, *That Hideous Strength* (New York: Scribner, 1996), 128.

6. Lewis, *That Hideous Strength*, 129.

7. Lewis, *That Hideous Strength*, 175.

8. Then we find an expanding lexicon of new words breaking mainstream—"Cisgender," "gender-fluid," "ze/zir," "birthing person," and "chestfeeding"—words invented by ideologues who work zealously to forever banish "oppressive" words like "mother," "father," "ladies," and "gentlemen" from human language. The plural third-person pronoun "they" to "refer to one person whose gender identity is nonbinary" was hailed as Merriam-Webster's Word of the Year in 2019.

9. Of women who seek abortions, 64 percent said they felt pressured by others, and more than half thought abortion was "morally wrong." Less than 1 percent said they felt better about themselves, 77.9 percent felt guilt, and 59.5 percent felt that "part of me died" (Vincent Rue et. al., "Induced Abortion and Traumatic Stress: A Preliminary Comparison of American and Russian Women," *Medical Science Monitor* 10, no. 10, October 2004: SR5–16, https:// pubmed.ncbi.nlm.nih.gov/15448616/). Women who have had abortions face an 81 percent increased risk of mental health problems (Priscilla Coleman, "Abortion and Mental Health: Quantitative Synthesis and Analysis of Research Published 1995– 2009," *British Journal of Psychiatry* 199, no. 3 (2011): 180–86, https:// doi.org/10.1192/bjp.bp.110.077230).

If our pursuit of justice does not include these women or take their harrowing stories seriously, then we just may be on the wrong side of history. See Sara Owens, "I Went to Planned Parenthood for Birth Control, but They Pushed Abortion," *The Federalist Society*, September 28, 2015, https://thefederalist.com/2015/09/28/i-went-to -planned-parenthood-for-birth-control-but-they-pushed-abortion.

Abortion was the leading cause of death worldwide in 2018,

tallying 42 million victims (Micaiah Bilger, "Abortion Was the Leading Cause of Death Worldwide, Tallying 42 Million," *Life News*, December, 31, 2018, https://www.lifenews.com/2018/12/31 /abortion-was-the-leading-cause-of-death-worldwide-in-2018 -killing-42-million-people/.)

In places such as Iceland, "the abortion rate for children diagnosed with Down syndrome approaches 100 percent" (George Will, "The Real Down-Syndrome Problem: Accepting Genocide," *Washington Post*, March 14, 2018, https://www.washingtonpost.com /opinions/whats-the-real-down-syndrome-problem-the-genocide /2018/03/14/3c4f8ab8–26ee-11e8-b79d-f3d931db7f68_story.html).

In the United States, 90 percent of preborn humans diagnosed with Down syndrome are terminated. In Asia, widespread sex-selective abortions have led to as many as 160 million "missing" women—more than the entire female population of the United States. Recent evidence suggests that sex-selective abortions of girls are common among certain populations in the United States as well; Caroline Mansfield, "Termination Rates after Prenatal Diagnosis of Down Syndrome, Spina Bifida, Anencephaly, and Turner and Klinefelter Syndromes: A Systematic Literature Review," *Prenatal Diagnosis* (September 22, 1999), https://pubmed.ncbi.nlm .nih.gov/10521836/; "Box v. Planned Parenthood of Indiana and Kentucky, Cornell Law School, retrieved on July 20, 2022, https:// www.law.cornell.edu/supremecourt/text/18–483.

If we are ok with these tiny humans being routinely exterminated because larger humans consider them inconvenient, genetically inferior, or too female, then we just may be on the wrong side of history.

10. George Orwell, *1984*.

11. As philosopher Paul Churchland stated it,

> The human species and all of its features are the wholly physical outcome of a purely physical process. . . . If this is the correct account of our origins, then there seems neither need, nor room, to fit any nonphysical substances or properties into our theoretical account of ourselves. We are creatures of matter. And we should learn to live with that fact. . . . Conscious intelligence is a wholly natural

phenomenon. . . . Conscious intelligence is the activity of
suitably organized matter, and the sophisticated organization responsible for it is, on this planet at least, the outcome
of billions of years of chemical, biological, and neurophysi-
ological evolution. (*Matter and Consciousness* [Cambridge,
MA: MIT Press, 1984], 21.)

As one of my least favorite songs of all time put it, "You and me
baby ain't nothin' but mammals, so let's do it like they do on the
Discovery Channel."

12. I explore this in more depth in chapter 4 of *Reflect: Becoming
Yourself by Mirroring the Greatest Person in History* (Bellingham,
WA: Lexham, 2018).

13. Richard Putnam, *Bowling Alone: The Collapse and Revival of
American Community* (New York: Simon & Schuster, 2000), 331,
emphasis in original.

14. Lisa Berkman and Leonard Syme, "Social Networks, Host
Resistance, and Mortality: A Nine-Year Follow-Up Study of
Alameda County Residents," *American Journal of Epidemiology* 109
(1979): 186–204.

15. See Charles Taylor, *A Secular Age* (Cambridge, MA: Harvard
University Press, 2007), 427.

16. David Foster Wallace, "This Is Water," commencement speech at
Kenyon College, 2005, https://fs.blog/david-foster-wallace-this
-is-water/.

17. "In 2021 We Tracked 733 Hate Groups Across the U.S.," Southern
Poverty Law Center, retrieved on July 20, 2022, https://www
.splcenter.org/states/california.

18. "Almost Half of Practicing Christian Millennials Say Evangelism Is
Wrong," Barna, February 15, 2019, https://www.barna.com
/research/millennials-oppose-evangelism/.

19. "Almost Half of Practicing Christian Millennials Say Evangelism Is
Wrong."

20. The Unthought also lies behind the relentless litigation against
charitable groups like the Little Sisters of the Poor and legislation
that would like to permanently close the doors of any school,
orphanage, crisis pregnancy center, hospital, or church that dares

question its doctrines. How have we been duped into thinking that such dogmatic aggression is somehow loving?

21. In Christian soteriology (doctrine of salvation) we find the doctrine of justification. Justification refers to, among other things, the divine act whereby God declares a sinner "not guilty!" on the basis of Christ's redemptive death and resurrection. God is the Judge, Satan is "the accuser," and Jesus is our Defense Attorney who appeals to his own completed death sentence so we can be declared not guilty. If we leave God out of the process of living free from guilt, then where must we turn for that authoritative declaration? We turn to the next biggest entity we can imagine. We turn to society, media, the law, education, entertainment, the local business owner—we must get *everyone* to declare us, in unison, "not guilty!" We must demonize and silence anyone who fails to acknowledge and celebrate our guiltlessness. The Little Sisters of the Poor, the baker, the photographer, and the Christian university become the collective functional equivalent to Satan and his minions in a historic Christian demonology.

22. Our definitions of love and hate don't spring into existence from some quantum vacuum. They come from our deeper worldview commitments, what Kuyper calls "two absolutely differing starting points"; *Lectures in Calvinism* (Grand Rapids: Eerdmans, 2009), 132. It all comes down to the question of whether we see man "in his present condition as normal, or as having fallen into sin, and having therefore become abnormal" (Kuyper, *Lectures in Calvinism*, 54). For abnormalists, like Jeremiah, Solomon, and Paul, the human heart is desperately sick, full of moral insanity, and dead in transgressions and sins (Jer. 17:9; Eccl. 9:3; Eph. 2:1). Those who recognize such abnormality "maintain the miraculous as the only means to restore the abnormal; the miracle of regeneration; the miracle of the Scriptures; the miracle in the Christ, descending as God with His own life into ours; and thus, owing to this regeneration of the abnormal, they continue to find the ideal norm not in the natural but in the Triune God" (Kuyper, *Lectures in Calvinism*, 132).

If, however, we are unfallen, then humanity "moves by means of an eternal evolution from its potencies to its ideal" (Kuyper,

Lectures in Calvinism, 132). This clarifies ways in which #loveislove has become a defining slogan of our generation. What is presupposed and then imposed is a normalist account of human nature. You must corroborate and celebrate my happiness as I currently conceive of happiness in all my unfallen perfection. Anything less is bigotry. From an abnormalist perspective, by contrast, love is not constricted to always say "be who you are." It can also say "become who you are" when that needs to be said. It is a love, like God's, that can passionately and zealously pursue the beloved's redemption and flourishing. Love can be redemptive only if we need redemption.

23. Alisa Childers, *Live Your Truth (and Other Lies): Exposing Popular Deceptions That Make Us Anxious, Exhausted, and Self Obsessed* (Carol Stream, IL: Tyndale Momentum, 2022), 162.

24. The preceding fictional dialogue was based on insights from Foucault himself along with his biographers, especially Roger Kimball, "The Perversions of M. Foucault," New Criterion, March 1993, https://newcriterion.com/issues/1993/3/the -perversions-of-m-foucault, and Warren Ward, *The Lovers of Philosophy* (UK: Ockham, 2022), ch. 4.

Epilogue: A Heretic's Manifesto

1. "Barna Omnipoll, August 2015," cited in David Kinnaman and Gabe Lyons, *Good Faith* (Grand Rapids: Baker, 2016), 58.

Index

Index

Index

Index

Schwartz, Barry, 188 n7

The Scream, 2, 199 n3. *See also* Munch,
Edvard

self-serving bias, 47–48, 112

self-worship,
as a religion, xiii–xvii, 9, 187 n10, 202 n1
devastation of, 60–64, 76, 137–138,
175–176, 193–194 n8
dullness of, 90–96
origins in Eden, 22–33
paradox of, 3
redefines love, 151–158, 168–169
robs us of awe, 7, 175
thought-leaders of, 60–64

Selma march, 79. *See also* King Jr., Martin
Luther; racism

sensory deprivation tanks, 4

sex, xiv, 28, 30, 40, 58–61, 111, 121, 151, 154,
159, 162–167, 196–197 n4. *See also* gender
theory; pedophilia; sexual revolution;
transgenderism

sexual revolution, 58, 61, 151, 165–167, 197
n5. *See also* Reich, Wilhelm; sex

shalom, 32

Shakespeare, xiv

Shiota, Michelle, 6, 188 n6. *See also* awe

Sigur Rós, 7

sin-killing, 112–113. *See also* Owen, John

Sinatra, Frank, xv

Siwa, JoJo, xv

Skywalker, Luke, 91, 93

Slaughterhouse-Five, 121. *See also* Vonnegut,
Kurt

Small Potatoes, 140. *See also* Disney

smart phone revolution, 22, 31, 60. *See also*
Jobs, Steve; social media

Smith, Sam, 29–30. *See also* gender fluidity;
transgenderism

"Snedronningen," 144. *See also* Anderson,
Hans Christian; *Frozen*

social media, 23, 31, 60, 61, 95, 152, 187 n10.
See also smart phone revolution

Solomon, 46, 155, 157, 211

Solzhenitsyn, Aleksandr, 89, 156, 157

Southern Poverty Law Center, 159

Spears, Britney, 81

Spector, Phil, 65. *See also* the Beatles

Sproul, R. C., 194 n10

Stanford Prison Experiment, 48. *See also*
Zimbardo, Philip

Steal this Book, 121. *See also* Hoffman, Abby

Suggested Language List, 153. *See also*
Brandheis University

suicide, 5, 47, 61, 64, 69

Swift, Taylor, 119, 141

Swinburne, A. C., 1

"Sympathy with the Devil," 29. *See also*
Rolling Stones

Tao, 41

Taylor, Charles, 204 n1

teleology, 145–147, 162. *See also* authored
life

Ten Commandments of Self-Worship,
xvi–xvii

That Hideous Strength, 153. *See also* Lewis,
C. S.

#theanswersarewithin, xvi, 103–113

theft, 32, 46, 78, 81, 95, 111, 121, 152

Thelema, 62. *See also* Crowley, Aleister

Themis (justice), 76, 83

theocracy, 161–162

Thirty Years War, 195 n13

This is Spinal Tap, 29

Thracians, 9

Three Miles North of Molkom, 206 n3

Thumbelina, xv

Thus Spoke Zarathustra, 66. *See also*
Nietzsche, Friedrich

TikTok, 66, 139. *See also* social media

"Time to be Awesome," 125. *See also* My
Little Pony: The Movie

Titian, 74–76, 83. *See also* Venus and the
Lute Player

Tolkien, J. R. R., 92, 115. *See also*
eucatastrophe

tolerance, 74, 81, 152, 159–160

toxic masculinity, 59

transgenderism, 139, 146, 162, 169–172, 208
n8. *See also* gender theory; Heyer, Walt;
Petras, Kim; sex

trans-specie-ism, 67. *See also* furries

Tree of Knowledge of Good and Evil,
23–28, 30. *See also* Adam and Eve; Satan;
self-worship

Trinity, 12, 16, 19, 109–110, 116, 127, 146,
176, 211 n22. *See also* Holy Spirit; Jesus

Tromsø, 4. *See also* awe

Trueman, Carl, 197 n5

Trump, Donald, 82

JOIN THE HERETICS

Be a part of the redemptive revolt against self-worship for the glory of God.

Sign the Heretic's Manifesto

WWW.JOINTHEHERETICS.COM

Confronting Injustice without Compromising Truth

12 Questions Christians Should Ask about Social Justice

Thaddeus J. Williams

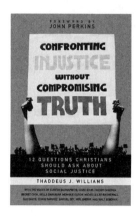

GOD DOES NOT SUGGEST, HE COMMANDS THAT WE FIGHT INJUSTICE

"The 12 questions Thaddeus raises in the book are the right questions we should all be asking in today's troubled world. Read with an open mind. Risk a change of heart. Don't get swept along into false answers that lead to only more injustice."

—John M. Perkins

"If you are a Christian concerned about oppression, injustice, racism, and other moral ills that plague our culture, there may not be a more important book you read this year."

—Alisa Childers

"This is the most important book I have recommended in over twenty years . . . the go-to resource for clear, biblical thinking about social justice."

—J. P. Moreland

In *Confronting Injustice without Compromising Truth*, Thaddeus Williams transcends our political tribalism and challenges readers to discover what the Bible and the example of Jesus have to teach us about justice. Drawing from a diverse range of theologians, sociologists, artists, and activists, Williams makes the case that we must be discerning if we are to "truly execute justice" as Scripture commands.

Not everything called "social justice" today is compatible with a biblical vision of a better world. With the help of twelve diverse contributors, Williams addresses topics like racism, sexuality, socialism, critical theory, and identity politics to present a compelling vision of justice for all God's image bearers that offers hopeful answers to life's biggest questions.